contents

striped pullover

Yarn
Any worsted weight cotton and acrylic blend yarn
- 17½oz/500g, 900yd/830m (17½oz/500g, 900yd/830m; 21oz/600g, 1090yd/990m; 21oz/600g, 1080yd/990m) in gray (A)
- 10½oz/300g, 540yd/500m (10½oz/300g, 540yd/500m; 14oz/400g, 720yd/660m; 14oz/400g, 720yd/660m) in blue (B)

Needles
- One pair each sizes 7 and 8 (4.5 and 5mm) needles *or size to obtain gauge*
- Two size 5 (3.75mm) double-pointed needles (dpns)

Notions
- Small stitch holders
- Stitch markers

SIZES
Sized for Small, Medium, Large, X-Large.
Shown in size Medium.

MEASUREMENTS
- **Chest** 42 (44, 46, 48)"/106.5 (111.5, 117, 122)cm.
- **Length** 26 (26½, 27, 27½)"/66 (67, 68.5, 70)cm.
- **Upper arm** 18 (18½, 19, 20)"/46 (47, 48, 51)cm.

GAUGE
17 sts and 24 rows to 4"/10cm over St st using larger needles.
Take time to check gauge.

STRIPE PATTERN
Working in St st, work *8 rows A, 6 rows B; rep from * (14 rows) for stripe pat.

BACK
With smaller needles and A, cast on 84 (88, 92, 96) sts. Work in k1, p1 rib for 2 rows. Change to larger needles and work in stripe pat for 18 rows.
Inc row (RS) K2, inc 1 st in next st, k to last 4 sts, inc 1 st in next st, k3.

Rep inc row every 18th row twice more—90 (94, 98, 102) sts.
Cont in stripe pat until there are 6 reps of the 14-row stripe pat, then work 8 rows with A once more. Piece measures approx 16"/40.5cm from beg.

Shape armhole
Bind off 4 sts at beg of next 2 rows, 2 sts at beg of next 2 rows.
Dec row (RS) K2, SKP, k to last 4 sts, k2tog, k2.
Rep dec row every other row 2 (3, 4, 5) times more—72 (74, 76, 78) sts.
Cont in stripe pat as established until there are a total of 8 B stripes. Discontinue stripe pat and cont to work with A only until armhole measures 8¾ (9¼, 9¾, 10¼)"/22 (23.5, 25, 26)cm, end with a WS row.
Place markers to mark the center 24 sts on the last WS row.

Shape shoulder and neck
Bind off 5 sts at beg of next 6 (8, 6, 4) rows, 4 (0, 6, 6) sts at beg of next 2 (0, 2, 4) rows, AT THE SAME TIME as the 3rd shoulder bind-off, bind off the center marked 24 sts, and working both sides at once, bind off 5 sts from each neck edge once.

FRONT
Work as for back, including the armhole shaping, until the 8th stripe in A is completed.
Mark the center 4 sts on the last WS row.

Separate for placket opening
Next row (RS) With B, work to the center marked sts, sl these 4 sts to a safety pin and join a 2nd ball of B, work to end.
Working both sides at once, complete the final stripe in B, then cont with A only until placket depth measures 4¼ (4¾, 5¼, 5¾)"/11 (12, 13.5, 14)cm.

Shape neck
From each neck edge, bind off 5 sts once, 3 sts once, 2 sts twice and 1 st 3 times—19 (20, 21, 22) sts rem each side.

Shape shoulder
Bind off 5 sts from each shoulder edge 3 (4, 3, 2) times, 4 (0, 6, 6) sts 1 (0, 1, 2) times.

SLEEVES
With smaller needles and A, cast on 43 (45, 47, 51) sts. Work in k1, p1 rib for 2 rows. Change to larger needles and cont in St st as foll:
Note Stripe pat will begin on a different row than the sweater body so that the stripes will match at the underarm.
Beg with 4 rows A, then work *6 rows B, 8 rows A; rep from * 7 times more, ending with 8 rows in A, AT THE SAME TIME, work sleeve shaping after 6 rows are worked above rib, as foll:
Inc row (RS) K2, inc 1 st in next st, k to last 4 sts, inc 1 st in next st, k3.
Rep inc row every 6th row 16 times more—77 (79, 81, 85) sts. Work even until stripe pat (as described above) is completed. Piece measures approx 19½"/49.5cm from beg.

Shape cap
Bind off 4 sts at beg of next 2 rows, 2 sts at beg of next 2 rows.
Note Cont to shape sleeve as foll, and when there are 10 B stripes, cont with A only to end of piece.
Dec row (RS) K2, SKP, k to last 4 sts, k2tog, k2.
Rep dec row every other row 8 (9, 10, 12) times more.
Bind off 4 sts at beg of next 4 rows, 5 sts at beg of next 2 rows. Bind off rem 21 sts.

Left placket
Return to the 4 sts on hold at the placket and join A to the right side of these sts. Using dpns, work as foll:
Row 1 (RS) *(P1, k1) into next st; rep from * to end—8 sts.
Row 2 (WS) Sl 1 wyif, k1, [p1, k1] 3 times.
Cont in k1, p1 rib until band fits along the left edge of the placket opening. Leave the 8 sts on hold and seam the placket edge to the left neck opening, adjusting rows if necessary. Leave sts on hold after seaming.

striped pullover

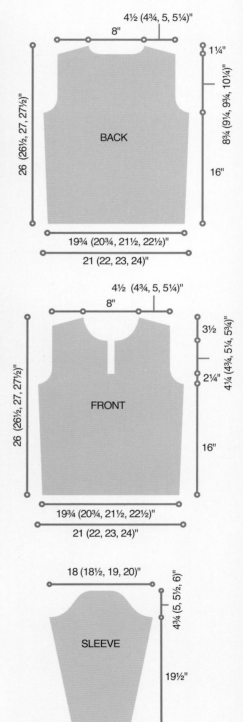

BACK

4½ (4¾, 5, 5¼)"
8"
1¼"
8¾ (9¼, 9¾, 10¼)"
16"
26 (26½, 27, 27½)"
19¾ (20¾, 21½, 22½)"
21 (22, 23, 24)"

FRONT

4½ (4¾, 5, 5¼)"
8"
3½
2¼"
4¼ (4¾, 5¼, 5¾)"
16"
26 (26½, 27, 27½)"
19¾ (20¾, 21½, 22½)"
21 (22, 23, 24)"

SLEEVE

18 (18½, 19, 20)"
4¾ (5, 5½, 6)"
19½"
10 (10½, 11, 12)"

Right placket

Working on the WS and at base of the left placket, pick up and k 8 sts along this line. Work right placket as for left placket, with a sl st on the outside edge. Seam as for left placket.

FINISHING

Do not block or steam pieces. Sew shoulder seams. Set in sleeves. Sew side and sleeve seams.

Neckband

With size 7 needles and A, pick up and k 122 sts evenly around neck edge, including sts from holders. Cont with the sl sts at beg and end, work in k1, p1 rib for 1¼"/3cm. Bind off in rib. ■

cabled scarf

Paul Amato for lvarepresents.com

Yarn
- 8¾oz/250g, 470yd/430m of any worsted weight wool yarn in red

Needles
- One pair size 9 (5.5mm) needles *or size to obtain gauge*

Notions
- Cable needle (cn)

SIZES
One size.

MEASUREMENTS
Approx 7 x 58"/18 x 147cm.

GAUGE
26 sts and 26 rows to 4"/10cm over reversible cable pat using size 9 (5.5mm) needles.
Take time to check gauge.

STITCH GLOSSARY
12-st RC Sl 6 sts to cn and hold to back, [k1, p1] 3 times, [k1, p1] 3 times from cn.

CABLE PATTERN
(multiple of 17 sts, plus 12)
Rows 1–6 *[K1, p1] 6 times, k5; rep from * to last 12 sts, [k1, p1] 6 times.
Row 7 *12-st RC, k5; rep from * to last 12 sts, 12-st RC.
Rows 8–13 Rep rows 1–6.
Rep rows 1–13 for cable pat.

SCARF
Cast on 46 sts. Work in cable pat until piece measures 58"/147cm from beg, end with a row 5 or 12. Bind off in pat. ■

ribbed cardigan

SIZES
Sized for Man's Small, Medium, Large, X-Large. Shown in size Medium.

MEASUREMENTS
• **Chest (buttoned)** 46 (48½, 53½, 56)"/116.5 (125, 136.5, 144.5)cm.
• **Length** 27½ (28, 28½, 29)"/69.5 (71, 72, 73.5)cm.
• **Upper arm** 18½ (19½, 20, 21)"/47 (49.5, 50.5, 53.5)cm.

GAUGE
16 sts and 22 rows to 4"/10cm over cartridge rib (slightly stretched) using larger needles.
Take time to check gauge.

K1, P1 RIB
(over an odd number of sts)
Row 1 *K1, p1; rep from *, end k1.
Row 2 K the knit sts and p the purl sts.
Rep row 2 for k1, p1 rib.

CARTRIDGE RIB
(over a multiple of 5 sts plus 2)
Row 1 (RS) K3, *p1, k4; rep from *, end last rep k3.
Row 2 *P2, k3; rep from *, end p2.
Rep rows 1 and 2 for cartridge rib.

BACK
With smaller needles, cast on 107 (113, 125, 131) sts. Work in k1, p1 rib for 3"/7.5cm, dec 15 (16, 18, 19) sts evenly across last (WS) row—92 (97, 107, 112) sts. Change to larger needles and work in cartridge rib until piece measures 17"/43cm from beg, end with WS row.

Shape armhole
Bind off 4 (4, 5, 5) sts at beg of next 2 rows, 2 (2, 3, 3) sts at beg of next 2 rows. Dec 1 st each side on next row, then every other row 3 (3, 4, 5) times more—72 (77, 81, 84) sts. Work even until armhole measures 9½ (10, 10½, 11)"/24 (25.5, 26.5, 28)cm, end with WS row.

Yarn 5
• 28oz/800g, 1280yd/1280m (29¾oz/850g, 1480yd/1360m; 33¼oz/950g, 1660yd/1530m; 35oz/1000g, 1740yd/1600m) of any bulky weight wool yarn in light brown

Needles
• One pair each sizes 10 and 10½(6 and 6.5mm) needles *or size to obtain gauge*

Notions
• Seven 1"/25mm buttons
• Stitch markers

Shape shoulder and neck
Bind off 7 (7, 9, 8) sts at beg of next 2 rows, 7 (8, 8, 9) sts at beg of next 4 rows. AT THE SAME TIME, bind off center 20 (21, 21, 22) sts and working both sides at once, bind off 5 sts from each neck edge once.

RIGHT FRONT
With smaller needles, cast on 57 (61, 67, 71) sts. Work in k1, p1 rib for 3"/7.5cm, dec 8 (8, 10, 10) sts on last (WS) row—49 (53, 57, 61) sts. Change to larger needles.

Beg cartridge rib
Next row (RS) Sl 1, work cartridge rib, ending k4 (3, 2, 1).
Next row Work rib to last st, p1. Cont as established until piece measures 17"/43cm from beg. Shape armhole at side edge (beg of WS rows, end of RS rows) same as back—39 (43, 44, 47) sts work 1 (WS) row even. Piece measures approx 19 (19, 19½, 19½)"/48 (48, 49.5, 49.5)cm from beg.

Shape neck
Row 1 (RS) Sl 1, k3, p1, k1, pm, SKP, k1, *p1, k4; rep from * to end.
Row 2 Work to 1 st before marker, p1, sl marker, k3, p3.
Row 3 Sl 1, k3, p1, k1, sl marker, SKP, *p1, k4; rep from * to end.
Row 4 Work to 1 st before marker, p1, sl marker, k3, p3.
Cont in this way to dec 1 st at neck edge, always working the dec'd st as p, every

other row 6 (8, 6, 9) times more, then every 4th row 6 (6, 7, 6) times—25 (27, 29, 30) sts. Work even until armhole measures 9½ (10, 10½, 11)"/24 (25.5, 26.5, 28)cm. Shape shoulder at side edge same as back. Bind off rem 4 sts. Place markers on front edge for 7 buttons, the first one at 1"/2.5cm from lower edge, the last one at beg of neck shaping and the other 5 spaced evenly between.

LEFT FRONT
With smaller needles, cast on 57 (61, 67, 71) sts. Work in k1, p1 rib for 1"/2.5cm, end with a WS row.
Buttonhole row (RS) Rib to last 5 sts, ssk, yo, work to end.
Next row P1, k1, p1, k into yo, cont rib to end. Cont in rib until piece measures 3"/7.5cm from beg, dec 8 (8, 10, 10) sts on last (WS) row—49 (53, 57, 61) sts. Change to larger needles.

Beg cartridge rib
Next row (RS) K4 (3, 2, 1), rep from * of cartridge rib to last st, k1. Next row Sl 1, work rib to end. Cont as established and work rem buttonholes opposite markers. Complete to correspond to right front, reversing all shaping by working armhole and shoulder bind-offs at beg of RS rows and work neck decs as foll:

Shape neck
Row 1 (RS) Work to last 8 sts, k2tog, pm, k1, p1, k4.
Row 2 Sl 1, p2, k3, sl marker, p1, *k3, p2; rep from * to end.
Row 3 Work to last 8 sts, k2tog, sl marker, k1, p1, k4.
Row 4 Sl 1, p2, k3, sl marker, p1, k2, p2, *k3, p2; rep from * to end.
Complete as for right front.

SLEEVES
With smaller needles, cast on 49 sts. Work in k1, p1 rib for 3"/7.5cm, dec 7 sts on last (WS) row—42 sts.
Change to larger needles and work in cartridge rib, inc 1 st each side (work-

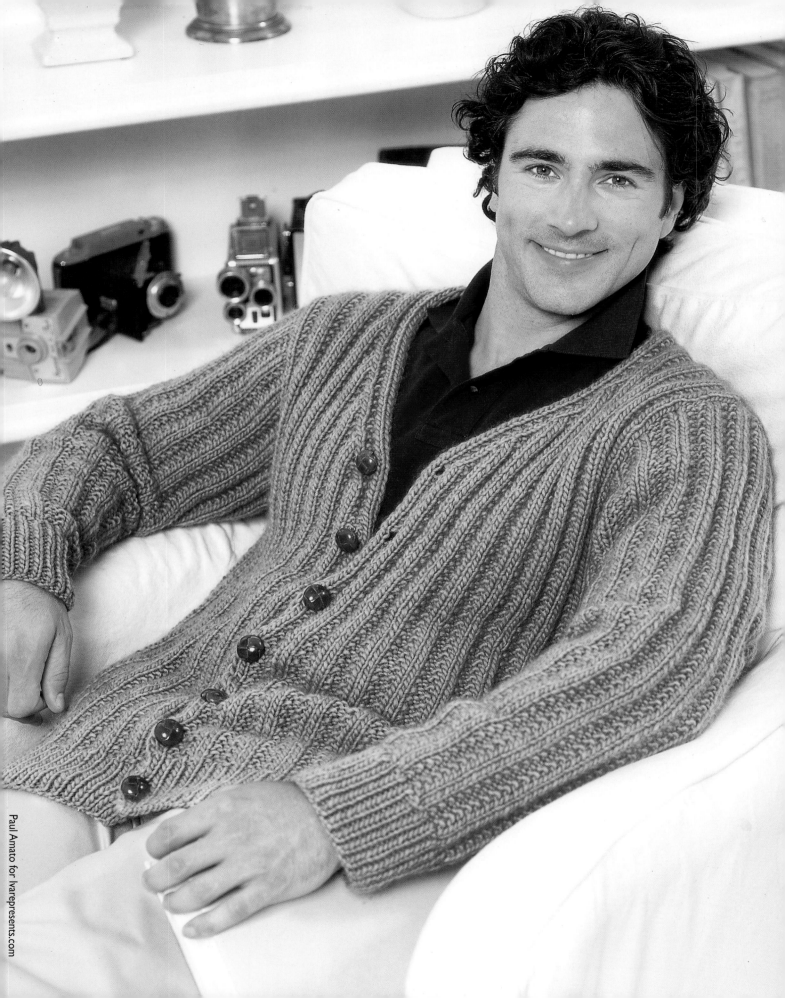

ribbed cardigan

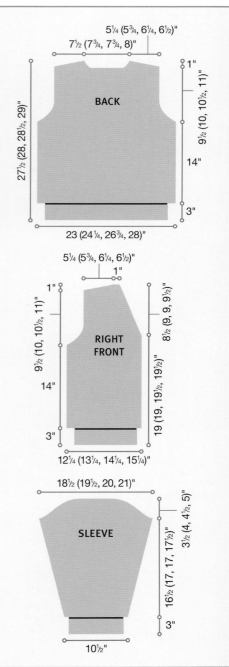

ing inc sts into pat) every 4th row 6 (10, 13, 18) times, every 6th row 10 (8, 6, 3) times––74 (78, 80, 84) sts. Work even until piece measures 19½ (20, 20, 20½)"/49.5 (50.5, 50.5, 52)cm from beg.

Shape cap
Bind off 4 (4, 5, 5) sts at beg of next 2 rows, 2 sts at beg of next 14 (16, 18, 26) rows, 4 (4, 3, 0) sts at beg of next 4 (4, 4, 0) rows. Bind off rem 22 sts.

FINISHING
Block pieces to measurements. Sew shoulder seams. Set in sleeves. Sew side and sleeve seams.

Back neckband
With RS facing and smaller needles, pick up and k 33 (35, 35, 37) sts evenly along back neck. Work in k1, p1 rib for 1"/2.5cm. Bind off in rib. Sew sides of band to 4 bound-off sts on front.
Sew buttons to right front, opposite buttonholes. ■

balaclava

SIZE
One size.

MEASUREMENTS
• **Head circumference** Approx 21"/53.5cm (stretched).
• **Length** 17"/43cm.

GAUGE
22 sts and 24 rows to 4"/10cm in k2, p2 rib (slightly stretched) using size 8 (5mm) needles.
Take time to check gauge.

BALACLAVA
With circular needle, cast on 120 sts for lower edge.

Join, taking care not to twist sts. Place marker for end of rnd and slip marker every rnd.
Next rnd (RS) *K2, p3, rep from * to end for k2, p3 rib.
Work in k2, p3 rib for 3"/7.5cm.
Next (dec) rnd *K2, p1, p2tog; rep from * around—96 sts.
Work in k2, p2 rib as established until piece measures 9"/23cm from beg.
Remove marker.

Face opening
Begin working back and forth as foll:
Row 1 (RS) K2, bind off 18 sts, ssk, cont rib to last 3 sts before bound-off sts, end k2tog, k1—76 sts.
Row 2 and all WS rows K the knit sts and p the purl sts.

Row 3 K1, ssk, cont rib to last 3 sts, end k2tog, k1—74 sts.
Row 5 K1, ssk, cont rib to last 3 sts, end k2tog, k1—72 sts.
Row 7 K1, ssk, cont rib to last 3 sts, end k2tog, k1—70 sts.
Row 9 K2, M1, cont rib to last 2 sts, end M1, k2—72 sts.
Row 11 K2, M1, cont rib to last 2 sts, end M1, k2—74 sts.
Row 13 K2, M1, cont rib to last 2 sts, end M1, k2—76 sts.
Row 15 K2, M1, cont rib to last 2 sts, M1, k2, cast on 18 sts, place marker—96 sts.
Join and cont to work k2, p2 rib in the round for 3½"/9cm.

Shape top
Next rnd *K2, p2tog, [k2, p2] 3 times, rep from * around—90 sts.
Next rnd *K2, p1, k2, p2tog, [k2, p2] twice, rep from * around—84 sts.
Next rnd *[K2, p1] twice, k2, p2tog, k2, p2; rep from * around—78 sts.
Next rnd *[K2, p1] 3 times, k2, p2tog, rep from * around—72 sts.
Work 3 rnds even in K2, p1 rib.
Change to dpns.
Next rnd *K1, ssk; rep from * around—48 sts.
Next rnd *K2tog; rep from * around—24 sts.
Cut yarn and thread through rem sts. Pull tightly to close. ■

Yarn (4)
• 4½oz/120g, 260yd/240m of any worsted weight wool yarn in navy or red

Needles
• Size 8 (5mm) circular needle, 16"/40cm long *or size to obtain gauge*
• One set (5) size 8 (5mm) double-pointed needles (dpns)

Notions
• Stitch marker

slip stitch hat

Yarn
- 3½oz/100g, 210yd/200m of any worsted weight wool yarn in variegated blue and brown

Needles
- One set (5) size 6 (4mm) double-pointed needles (dpns) *or size to obtain gauge*

Notions
- Stitch marker

SIZE
One size.

MEASUREMENTS
- **Circumference** 21"/53.5cm.
- **Height** 7½"/19cm.

GAUGE
21 sts and 32 rows to 4"/10cm over sl stitch pat using size 6 (4mm) needles. *Take time to check gauge.*

SLIP STITCH PAT
(over multiples of 8)
Rnd 1 Knit.
Rnd 2 *K5, sl 3 purlwise wyif; rep from * to end.
Rep rnds 1 and 2 for sl stitch pat.

HAT
Cast on 7 sts. Place marker and join for knitting in the round, taking care not to twist sts.
Rnd 1 *Kfb; rep from * around—14 sts.
Rnds 2, 4 and 6 Knit.
Rnd 3 *Kfb; rep from * around—28 sts.
Rnd 5 *K1, kfb; rep from * around—42 sts.
Rnd 7 *K2, kfb; rep from * around—56 sts.
Rnd 8 *K3, sl 1 purlwise wyif; rep from * around.
Rnd 9 *K3, kfb; rep from * around—70 sts.
Rnd 10 *K3, sl 2 purlwise wyif; rep from * around.
Rnd 11 K3, *kfb, k4; rep from * to last 2 sts before marker, kfb, k1—84 sts.

Rnd 12 *K4, sl 2 purlwise wyif; rep from * around.
Rnd 13 *K5, kfb; rep from * around—98 sts.
Rnd 14 *K4, sl 3 purlwise wyif; rep from * around.
Rnd 15 K4, *kfb, k6; rep from * to last 3 sts before marker, kfb, k2—112 sts.
Rnd 16 *K5, sl 3 purlwise wyif; rep from * around.
Rnd 17 Knit.

Rep rnds 16 and 17 for sl st pat until piece measures 6½"/16.5cm from beg.
Next rnd * K2, p2; rep from * around for k2, p2 rib.
Work in k2, p2 rib for 1"/2.5cm.
Bind off in rib. ■

Paul Amato for lvarepresents.com

"hers" sweater

Yarn

Any bulky weight wool yarn
- 21oz/600g, 660yd/610m (24½oz/700g, 770yd/710m; 28oz/800g, 880yd/810m; 29¾oz/850g, 940yd/860m) in black (A)
- 10½oz/300g, 330yd/310m (12¼oz/350g, 390yd/360m; 14oz/400g, 440yd/410m; 15¾oz/450g, 500yd/460m) in gray (B)
- 5¼oz/150g, 170yd/160m in burgundy (C)

Needles
- One pair size 10½ (6.5mm) needles *or size to obtain gauge*
- Size 10 (6mm) circular needle, 16"/40cm long

SIZES

Sized for Man's Small (Medium, Large, X-Large). Shown in size Small.

MEASUREMENTS
- **Chest** 44 (48, 52, 56)"/112 (122, 132, 142)cm.
- **Length** 26½ (27½, 29, 30½)"/67 (69.5, 73.5, 77.5)cm.
- **Upper arm** 17 (18¼, 19½, 20½)"/43 (46.5, 49.5, 52)cm.

GAUGE

14 sts and 22 rows to 4"/10cm over St st using size 10 (6mm) needles.
Take time to check gauge.

NOTES

1 When working chart for the "Hers" band pat, carry color not in use loosely across back of work and twist around working color to prevent holes in work.
2 The cast-on st in A above the slit is a selvage st used for seaming.

BACK

With C, cast on 79 (85, 91, 97) sts.
Row 1 (RS) *K1, p1; rep from *, end sl 1 knitwise wyib.
Row 2 *P1, k1; rep from *, end sl 1 purlwise wyif.
Rep these 2 rows for rib twice more.

Next row (RS) Work 3 sts in rib as established with C, join A, and k 73 (79, 85, 91), join C, and rib 3 sts. Cont to work in St st with A and in rib as established with C, until piece measures 4"/10cm from beg. Cut C and cont in St st over all sts with A only until piece measures 17½ (18, 18½, 19½)"/44.5 (45.5, 47, 49.5)cm from beg, end with a WS row.

Shape armhole

Bind off 2 sts at beg of next 4 (4, 4, 6) rows.
Dec row (RS) K1, k2tog, k to last 3 sts, SKP, k1.

Rep dec row every other row 3 (4, 5, 5) times more—63 (67, 71, 73) sts. Work even until armhole measures 8 (8½, 9½, 10)"/20.5 (21.5, 24, 25.5)cm, end with a WS row.

Shape neck and shoulder

Bind off 5 (5, 7, 6) sts at beg of next 2 rows, 5 (6, 6, 7) sts at beg of next 4 rows, AT THE SAME TIME, join a 2nd ball of yarn and bind off center 25 sts and working both sides at once with separate balls of yarn, bind off 2 sts from each neck edge twice.

"hers" sweater

FRONT

Work as for back until piece measures approx 16 (16½, 17, 18)"/40.5 (42, 43, 45.5) cm from beg OR 9 rows less than back to armhole shaping, end with a RS row.

Beg stripe pattern

Beg with a purl row, work 1 row B, [1 row A, 1 row C] twice, 2 rows B, 2 rows A. Mark center 42 stitches

Shape armhole

With B, work to marker, sl marker, work 42-st chart pat, sl marker, with B work to end. Work chart in this way through row 11. AT THE SAME TIME, shape the armhole as on back. When chart is completed, work 2 rows A, 2 rows B, [1 row C, 1 row A] twice, 1 row B, 1 row A, then cont with B on 63 (67, 71, 73) sts after all shaping until armhole measures 6 (6½, 7½, 8)"/15 (16.5, 19, 20.5)cm.

Shape neck

Next row (RS) K24 (26, 28, 29) sts, join a 2nd ball of yarn and bind off center 15 sts, k to end. Working both sides at once with separate balls of yarn, bind off 3 sts from each neck edge once.
Neck dec row (RS) Work to last 4 sts of first side, k2tog, k2; on 2nd side, k2, SKP, k to end.
Neck dec row (WS) P to last 4 sts of first side, p2tog tbl, p2; on 2nd side p2, p2tog, p to end. Rep the last 2 rows twice more—15 (17, 19, 20) sts rem each side. Work even until armhole measures same as on back.

Shape shoulder

From each shoulder edge, bind off 5 (5, 7, 6) sts once, 5 (6, 6, 7) sts twice.

SLEEVES

With C, cast on 40 (44, 46, 48) sts.
Next row *K1, p1; rep from * to end.
Next row K the knit sts and p the purl sts for k1, p1 rib.

Cont in k1, p1 rib for 4 rows more. Change to B and cont in St st, inc 1 st each side every 8th row 10 (10, 11, 12) times—60 (64, 68, 72) sts. Work even until piece measures 20½ (20½, 21, 21½)"/52 (52, 53, 54.5) cm from beg.

Shape cap

Bind off 7 sts at beg of next 2 rows.
Dec row (RS) K1, k2tog, k to last 3 sts, SKP, k1.
Rep dec row every other row 5 times. Bind off 4 sts at beg of next 4 rows. Bind off rem 18 (22, 26, 30) sts.

FINISHING

Block pieces to measurements. Sew shoulder seams. Set in sleeves. Sew sleeve seams. Sew side seams, leaving the lower C trimmed slit free.

Neckband

With RS facing, circular needle and C, pick up and k 74 sts evenly around neck edge. Join, pm to mark beg of rnd. Work in rnds of k1, p1 rib for 7 rnds. Bind off. ■

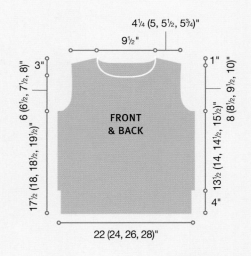
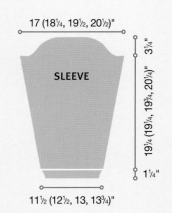
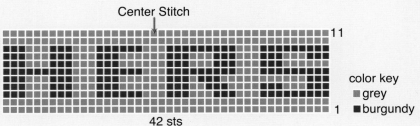

Rose Callahan

navy vest

Yarn
- 24½oz/700g, 700yd/640m (28oz/800g, 800yd/730m; 28oz/800g, 800yd/730m; 31½oz/900g, 900yd/820m; 31½oz/900g, 900yd/820m) of any worsted weight wool yarn in navy

Needles
- One pair each sizes 9 and 10½ (5.5 and 6.5mm) needles *or size to obtain gauge*
- Size 9 (5.5mm) circular needle, 16"/40cm long

Notions
- Safety pin or stitch holder

SIZES
Sized for Man's Small (Medium, Large, XL, XXL). Shown in size Small.

MEASUREMENTS
- **Chest** 38 (40, 42, 44, 46)"/95.5 (101.5, 106.5, 111.5, 117)cm.
- **Length** 29 (29½, 30½, 32, 33)"/73.5 (75, 77.5, 81, 84)cm.

GAUGE
15 sts and 24 rows to 4"/10cm over mock rib stitch using larger needles.
Take time to check gauge.

MOCK RIB STITCH
(over an odd number of sts)
Row 1 (RS) P1, *wyib, sl 1 purlwise, yarn to front, p1; rep from * to end.
Row 2 Purl.
Rep rows 1 and 2 for mock rib st.

BACK
With smaller needles, cast on 63 (67, 71, 75, 79) sts.
Row 1 (RS) P1, *k1, p1; rep from * to end. K the knit sts and p the purl sts for k1, p1 rib for 3"/7.5cm, end with a WS row. Change to larger needles. Beg with row 1, work in mock rib st, inc 1 st each side (in pat) every 12th row 4 times—71 (75, 79, 83, 87) sts. Work even until piece measures 19 (19, 19½, 20, 20½)"/48 (48, 49.5, 51, 52)cm from beg.

Shape armhole
Bind off 4 (4, 5, 5, 5) sts at beg of next 2 rows.
Dec row (RS) K0 (0, 1, 1, 1), p1, SK2P, work in pat to last 4 (4, 5, 5, 5) sts, k3tog, p1, k0 (0, 1, 1, 1). Rep dec row every 4th row 1 (2, 2, 2, 2) times more—55 (55, 57, 61, 65) sts. Work even until armhole measures 8½ (9, 9½, 10½, 11)"/21.5 (23, 24, 26.5, 28)cm.

Shape shoulder
Bind off 4 sts at beg of next 8 (8, 6, 4, 0) rows, 5 sts at beg of next 0 (0, 2, 4, 8) rows. Bind off rem 23 (23, 23, 25, 25) sts.

FRONT
Work as for back to the armhole.

Shape armhole
Work as for back—55 (55, 57, 61, 65) sts. Work even until armhole measures 1½ (2, 2½, 3½, 4)"/4 (5, 6.5, 9, 10)cm.

Shape neck
Next row (RS) Work 27 (27, 28, 30, 32) sts, sl center st to a safety pin, join a 2nd ball of yarn and work to end. Work both sides at once for 1 row on WS.
Dec row (RS) Work to the last 4 sts of first side, k3tog, p1; on 2nd side, p1, SK2P, work to end. Rep dec row every 6th row 4 (4, 4, 5, 5) times more—17 (17, 18, 18, 20) sts rem each side. Work even until armhole measures same as back to shoulder; dec 1 (1, 1, 0, 0) st at neck edge on last row. Work shoulder shaping as on back.

FINISHING
Do not block. Sew shoulder seams.

Armhole trim
With smaller needles, pick up and k 80 (84, 90, 96, 100) sts evenly around armhole edge. Work in k1, p1 rib for 1½"/4cm. Bind off in rib. Sew side seams.

Neckband
With circular needle, pick up and k 113 (113, 113, 117, 117) sts evenly around neck edge, including center st from safety pin. Join to work in rnds, pm to mark beg of rnd.
Rnd 1 Work in k1, p1 rib to 2 sts before center st, SKP, k1 (center st), k2tog, rib to end. Rep this rnd every rnd until neckband measures 1½"/4cm. Bind off in rib. ■

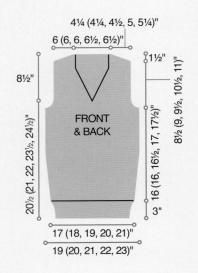

ribbed cap

SIZE
One size.

MEASUREMENTS
- **Head circumference** 21"/53cm.
- **Length** 8"/20.5cm.

GAUGE
20 sts and 32 rnds to 4"/10cm over St st using size 6 (4mm) needles.
Take time to check gauge.

PATTERN STITCH
(multiple of 7 sts)
Rnd 1 *K1, p1, k2, p3; rep from * around.
Rnds 2 and 4 K the knit sts and p the purl sts.
Rnd 3 *K2, p1, k1, p3; rep from * around.
Rep rnds 1–4 for pat st.

HAT
Brim
With MC, cast on 105 sts. Join and pm, being careful not to twist sts. Work in pat st until piece measures 7"/18cm from beg.

Shape crown
Next (dec) rnd *Work in pat over next 3 sts, SKP, p2; rep from * around—90 sts. Work 1 rnd even.
Next (dec) rnd Work in pat over 4 sts, *p1, k2tog, work in pat over 3 sts; rep from * around, working last st of rnd tog with first st of next rnd, keep this st as first st of

rnd—75 sts. Work 1 rnd even.
Next (dec) rnd *Work 3 sts in pat, SKP; rep from * around—60 sts.
Next (dec) rnd *K1, p2tog, k1; rep from * around—45 sts.
Next (dec) rnd Work 2 sts in pat, *SKP, p1; rep from * around, work last SKP with first st of next rnd—30 sts.
Next (dec) rnd P1, *SKP; rep from * around, work last SKP with first st of next rnd—15 sts.
Next (dec) rnd K1, *SKP; rep from * around—8 sts. Cut yarn leaving long tail.

Thread through yarn needle and draw through rem sts.

FINISHING
With crochet hook, CC and WS facing sl st in one lp of each cast-on st around. Join with sl st and fasten off. ■

plaid scarf

Paul Amato

Yarn [5]
Any bulky weight acrylic and wool blend yarn
- 10oz/280g, 310yd/290m each in cream and brown
- 5oz/140g, 160yd/150m each in orange and black

Needles
- One pair size 10½ (6.5mm) needles *or size to obtain gauge*

Notions
- Size K/10½ (7mm) crochet hook.

SIZE
One size.

MEASUREMENTS
Approx 9"/23cm wide × 80"/203cm long (excluding fringe).

GAUGE
12 sts and 18 rows to 4"/10cm over St st using size 10½ (6.5mm) needles.
Take time to check gauge.

NOTE
The 3 vertical stripes in orange, black and orange will be worked in the designated p-stitch ribs in chain-stitch using a crochet hook after scarf is completed.

SCARF
Using cream, cast on 27 sts.
*Row 1 (RS) [K6, p1] 3 times, k6.
Row 2 Knit.
Rows 3 and 5 Rep row 1.
Rows 4 and 6 Knit.*

Beg chart
Beg with row 1 of chart, work 27 sts of chart, rep rows 1–36 for a total of 10 times, then working chart in reverse, work rows 20–1 once.

Rep between *'s (the first 6 rows) once. Piece measures approx 80"/203cm from beg. Bind off.

Vertical stripes
Locating 7th (purl) st from RH edge, using orange and crochet hook, work chain stitch (with yarn at back of work), working 1 chain st in every garter ridge (or covering 2 rows) and 1 chain st in every St st row. With black, work center stripe in same way. With orange, work 3rd stripe in same way.

Fringe
Cut three 16"/40cm lengths of orange for each fringe.
Place 3 fringes in each of the 4 sections (for a total of 12 fringes) on each short end of scarf.
Knot fringe with knot showing on RS. ■

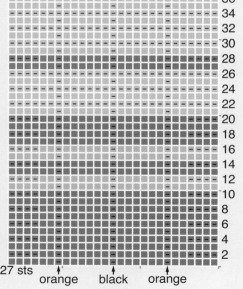

27 sts   ↑ orange   ↑ black   ↑ orange

K on RS, P on WS
key ■ brown ▨ orange ▧ cream ■ black
P on RS, K on WS
▤ brown − orange − cream ▬ black

cuban shirt

SIZE

Sized for one size, Man's Medium/Large.

MEASUREMENTS

• **Chest** 44"/112cm.
• **Length** 25"/63.5cm.
• **Upper arm** 21½"/54.5cm.

GAUGE

16 sts and 20 rows to 4"/10 cm over St st using larger needles.
Take time to check gauge.

STITCH GLOSSARY

HDC (half double crochet) Yo, insert hook and draw up a loop, yo and pull through 3 lopps on hook.

NOTE

Shirt is made in pieces and then put tog using a crochet hook with hdc through the selvage of one piece then hdc through the selvage of the adjacent piece. A portion of the shoulder of the back yoke wraps around to the front.

BACK YOKE

Note This piece is worked from side to side. With larger needles and MC, beg at the left back shoulder edge, cast on 21 sts.
Row 1 (WS) Purl.
Row 2 (RS) Sl 2 wyib, k to the last 2 sts, M1, (for shoulder), k2.
Row 3 Sl 2 purlwise wyif, purl to end.
Row 4 Sl 2, k to end.
Row 5 Rep row 3.
Rep rows 2–5 8 times more—30 sts.
Rows 38–40 Work even.

Shape neck

Row 41 (WS) Bind off 10 sts, purl to end.
Row 42 Sl 2, k to last 3 sts, ssk, k1.
Row 43 Sl 2, purl to end.
Rows 44–47 Rep rows 42 and 43 twice more—17 sts. Work even for 14 rows.
Row 62 Sl 2, k to last 2 sts, M1, k2.
Row 63 Sl 2, purl to end.

Yarn 4
Any worsted weight linen yarn
• 14oz/400g, 760yd/700m in medium brown (MC)
• 3½oz/100g, 190yd/180m each in yellow (A), cream (B), and charcoal (C)

Needles
• One pair each sizes 4 and 7 (3.5 and 7.5mm) needles *or size to obtain gauge*
• One size 4 (3.5mm) circular needle, 24"/60cm length

Notions
• One each crochet hook sizes D/3 and J/10 (3.25 and 6mm)
• Six ¾"/19mm and six ⅝"/16mm buttons
• Stitch markers

Rep rows 62 and 63 twice more. Work even for 2 rows.
Row 70 Sl 2, k to end, cast on 10 sts at end of row—30 sts.

Shape right shoulder

Row 71 Sl 2, p to end.
Row 72 Sl 2, k to last 3 sts, ssk, k1.
Row 73 Rep row 71.
Row 74 Sl 2, k to end. Rep rows 71–74 8 times more—21 sts. Work 1 row even. Bind off.

BACK

Place markers at 19-st intervals on lower edge of back yoke to mark 3 even back panels to indicated placement of the crochet seam. With smaller circular needles and MC, *pick up and k 25 sts to marker; rep from * twice more.
Row 1 (WS) Purl.

Work left back

Row 2 With larger needles, sl 2, p2, k17, p2, k2, turn, leaving the rem sts on hold.
Row 3 Sl 2, p23. Rep the last 2 rows 16 times more.

Shape armhole

Row 36 Sl 2, M1, p2, work to end.
Row 37 Sl 2, purl to end. Rep the last 2 rows 3 times more—29 sts.

Row 44 Sl 2, k4, p2, k17, p2, k2.
Row 45 Sl 2, purl to end. Rep the last 2 rows until side seam measures approx 16"/40.5cm from armhole. Leave sts on hold.

Work center back

Row 2 Sl 2, p2, k6, yo, k2tog, k1, ssk, yo, k6, p2, k2.
Row 3 Sl 2, purl to end. Rep rows 2 and 3 until center back measures same as back as the left back. Leave sts on hold.

Work right back

Work as for left back, reversing shaping.

LEFT FRONT

Place a marker at center of the left front shoulder upper edge of back yoke piece to mark 2 equal panels. With smaller needles and MC, pick up and k 15 sts from marker to the outer (armhole) edge. Purl 1 row.

Work outer left panel

Row 2 (RS) With larger needles, sl 2, k11, p2.
Row 3 Sl 2, p13. Rep the last 2 rows 27 times more.
Row 57 Sl 2, k to last 2 sts, p2, inc 1 k st.
Row 58 Sl 2, purl to end.
Rep the last 2 rows 3 times more—19 sts. Work even until there are a total of 148 rows from beg and side seam measures same as back. Leave sts on hold.

Work openwork panel

With smaller needles and MC, pick up and k 15 rem sts along the shoulder edge to marker. Purl 1 row. Change to larger needles and A.
Row 2 (RS) Sl 2, k13.
Row 3 and all WS rows Sl 2, p13.
Row 4 Sl 2, p3, k2tog, M1, k1, M1, ssk, p3, k2.
Row 6 Sl 2, p2, k2tog, k1, yo, k1, yo, k1, ssk, p2, k2.
Row 8 Sl 2, p1, k2tog, k1, yo, k3, yo, k1, ssk, p1, k2.
Row 10 Sl 2, k2tog, k1, yo, k5, yo, k1, ssk, k2.
Row 12 Sl 2, yo, k1, ssk, k5, k2tog, k1, yo, k2.
Row 14 Sl 2, p1, yo, k1, ssk, k3, k2tog, k1, yo, p1, k2.

Paul Amato

cuban shirt

Row 16 Sl 2, p2, yo, k1, ssk, k1, k2tog, k1, yo, p2, k2.

Row 18 Sl 2, p3, yo, k1, S2KP, k1, yo, p3, k2.

Row 19 Rep row 3. Rep rows 4–19 for 8 times more.

Row 148 Sl 2, p4, k3, p4, k2. Leave sts on hold.

CENTER PANEL

With larger needles and MC, cast on 5 sts.

Row 1 (WS) Purl.

Row 2 Sl 2, M1, k3.

Row 3 Sl 2, p4.

Row 4 Sl 2, M1, k to end.

Row 5 Sl 2, purl to end.

Rep the last 2 rows 3 times more—10 sts.

Row 12 (RS) Cast on 11 sts (for neck edge), k to end—21 sts.

Row 13 Sl 2, purl to end.

Row 14 Sl 2, k1, [p1, k1] 5 times, k8.

Row 15 Sl 2, p6, [p1, k1] 5 times, p3.

Row 16 Sl 2, p1, [k1, p1] 5 times, k8.

Row 18 Sl 2, p6, [k1, p1] 5 times, p3.

Rep the last 4 rows until there are a total of 148 rows from beg and piece measures same as other panels. Leave sts on hold. Place markers for 6 buttons, the first one at ¾"/2cm from top, the last one at 5"/12.5cm from bottom and the others evenly spaced between.

RIGHT FRONT

Work as for left front, reversing all shaping and forming 6 buttonholes opposite markers by binding off 3 sts for each buttonhole at 4 sts from center front edge on the first row and casting on 3 sts over the bound-off sts on the 2nd row.

SLEEVES

With RS facing, smaller needles and MC, pick up and k 85 sts along the entire armhole edge.

Row 1 (WS) P2, *p2tog, yo; rep from * to last 5 sts, p3tog, yo, p2. Change to larger needles.

Row 2 Sl 2, k to end.

Row 3 Sl 2, p to end.

Dec row 4 Sl 2, k2tog, k to last 4 sts, ssk, k2.

Cont in St st, rep dec row every 4th row 7 times more—69 sts. Change to A and work 4 rows more in St st. K next WS row for turning ridge and cont in St st for 3 rows more. Bind off.

COLLAR

With larger crochet hook and A, work an edge of sl st all around the neck edge to make the edge firm. With smaller needles and A, working the WS of the garment (and RS of the collar), beg at 1½"/4cm from beg and end of neck edge, pick up and k 62 sts along the neck edge.

Row 1 (WS) Purl. Change to larger needles.

Row 2 Sl 2, knit to end.

Row 3 Sl 2, purl to end.

Inc row 4 Sl 2, M1, k to last 2 sts, M1, k2. Cont in St st, rep inc row every 4th row 3 times more—70 sts. Work 4 rows even. Change to B.

Row 21 Purl.

Row 22 K1, k2tog, *yo, k2tog; rep from * to last 3 sts, yo, k2tog, k1.

Row 23 Purl.

Dec row 24 Sl 2, k2tog, k to last 4 sts, ssk, k2. Cont in St st, rep dec row every 4th row 3 times more—62 sts. Work 2 rows even. Bind off. Fold collar along the picot edge and sew collar to neck edge. Sew side edges to collar tog.

JOIN PANELS

All panels and seams are joined by working 1 hdc with smaller hook in the selvage st on first panel to be joined, then 1 hdc on the adjacent panel. At the end of the joined pieces, ch 2 and join at end, then fasten off.

Use B to join the front panels on 2 sides. Use C to join the back panels for the side seams, and sleeve seams, leave a 4"/10cm side slit and join with C for the side seam and through the sleeve seam.

FINISHING

Turn the sleeve cuff hems to WS and sew in place.

Make facings

For the back facing, with larger needles and C, pick up and k 79 sts from the back edge. Work in St st for 8 rows. Bind off. Work front facings by picking up 51 sts and work in same way. With smaller hook and C, work 1 sl st all around the slits and lower edges. Sew on large buttons opposite buttonholes. Sew on the smaller button to the WS to secure the top button in place. Block the finished garment flat. ■

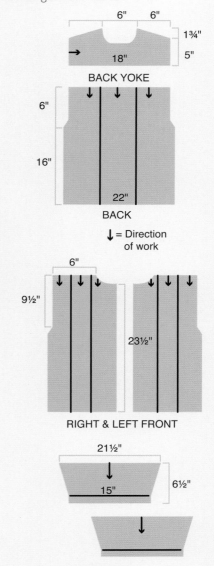

BACK YOKE
6" 6"
1¾"
18"
5"

BACK
6"
16"
22"

↓ = Direction of work

RIGHT & LEFT FRONT
6"
9½"
23½"

SLEEVES
21½"
15"
6½"

argyle scarf

Paul Amato for Ivarepresents.com

Yarn
- 5oz/140g, 160yd/150m of any bulky weight wool and acrylic blend yarn each in green, cream, orange and purple

Needles
- One pair size 10 (6mm) needles *or size to obtain gauge*
- Bobbins (optional)

SIZE
One size.

MEASUREMENTS
Approx 9"/23cm x 33"/83.5cm, not including fringe.

GAUGE
15 sts and 22 rows to 4"/10cm over St st and chart pat using size 10 (6mm) needles.
Take time to check gauge.

NOTES
1 Use separate bobbins for each color section and twist strands on WS at color change to prevent holes.

2 Purple sts on chart can be knit in or worked in duplicate stitch after scarf is knit.

SCARF
With green, cast on 33 sts. Work in St st, working rows 1–28 of chart pat 7 times. Bind off with green.

FINISHING
If purple sts were not knit in, duplicate stitch them on scarf following the chart for placement. Pin block into shape.

Fringe
Cut strands of each color approx 7"/17.5cm long. Using 1 strand for each fringe, attach 1 fringe in each cast-on and bound-off st at end of scarf, matching the colors of the argyle pattern. ■

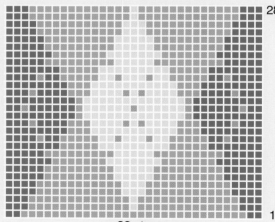

28

1

33 sts

color key
- green
- cream
- orange
- purple

peruvian hat

Yarn
- 3oz/85g, 200yd/190m of any worsted weight wool and acrylic blend yarn each in blue (A), green (B), cranberry (C), brown (D) and gold (E)

Needles
- One set (5) size 8 (5mm) double-pointed needles (dpns) *or size to obtain gauge*

Notions
- Yarn needle
- Stitch marker

SIZE
One size.

MEASUREMENTS
- **Length (top point to lower edge of ear flap)** 21"/53.5cm.
- **Circumference** 22"/56cm.

GAUGE
18 sts and 24 rows to 4"/10 cm over St st using size 8 (5mm) needles.
Take time to check gauge.

EAR FLAPS
With D and 2 needles only, cast on 5 sts.
Rows 1–22 Work in St st, working back and forth on 2 needles, foll chart 1 for shaping and color changes—25 sts. Cut A, but do not bind off. Set needle with 25 sts aside. Make a 2nd ear flap in same way.

CROWN
Note Crown is worked in rnd in St st (knit every rnd).
Rnd 1 (RS) Join D and k25 across 2nd ear flap; cast 25 sts onto an empty dpn; k25 across first ear flap; cast 25 sts onto a 4th empty dpn, join, being careful not to twist sts and place marker for beg of rnd—100 sts, 25 sts on each of 4 dpns.
Rnds 2 and 3 *K5 with D; k5 with C; rep from * around.

Paul Amato for lla represent.com

Rnds 4–26 Work chart 2 (work 25-st rep 4 times).
Rnd 27 *With D, k5; with A, k5; rep from * around.
Rnd 28 (Dec rnd) *With D, k3, k2tog; with A, k3 k2tog; rep from * around—80 sts, 20 sts on each of 4 dpns.
Rnds 29–52 Work chart 3 (work 20-st rep 4 times).
Rnd 53 With B, k4; with E, k4; rep from * around.
Rnd 54 (Dec rnd) *With B, k2, k2tog; with

E, k2, k2tog; rep from * around—60 sts, 15 sts on each of 4 dpns.
Rnds 55–72 Work chart 7 (work 15-st rep 4 times).
Rnd 73 *With E, k3; with D, k3; rep from * around.
Rnd 74 (Dec rnd) *With E, k1, k2tog; with D, k1, k2tog; rep from * around—40 sts, 10 sts on each of 4 dpns.
Rnds 75–84 Work chart 5 (work 10-st rep 4 times).
Rnd 85 With A, knit.

Rnd 86 (Dec rnd) *With A, k2tog; rep from * around—20 sts, 5 sts on each of 4 dpns.
Rnds 87–88 and 91–92 With C, knit.
Rnds 89–90 With A, knit. Cut yarn, leaving an 18"/45cm yarn end. Using yarn needle, thread yarn end through rem sts and draw tightly to close last rnd. Secure yarn end.

FINISHING
Joined i-cord edging
Using one dpn, cast on 3 sts with A. Using same dpn and starting at center back, pick up and k, 1 st in edge of hat, using another dpn, pass next-to-last st on RH needle over picked-up st; slide rem sts to opposite end of needle; *k2, sl 1 purlwise, using RH

needle pick up and k next st on edge of hat, pass next-to-last st on RH needle over picked-up st, slide rem 3 sts to opposite end of needle; rep from * around entire lower edge of hat. Cut yarn, leaving a yarn end for sewing; draw yarn end through last 3 sts on needle; sew to first 3 sts of edging.

Ties
With C, pick up 3 sts at tip of ear flap with one dpn, *k3, slide sts to opposite end of dpn; rep from * until tie is 12"/30.5 cm long. Cut yarn, leaving a 4"/10cm yarn end for sewing. Sew last rnd of tie to a point 2"/5 cm from end of tie to form a 1"/2.5cm loop. Weave yarn end into tie and trim.

Tassel
Hold 2 strands of each color tog (10 strands total) and wrap 7 times around a 6"/15cm piece of cardboard. Cut the end of the wrapping strand and then all strands along same edge of cardboard. Cut two 12"/30.5cm lengths of any color yarn and wrap them around the center of all strands twice and tie a firm knot. Trim tassel ends. Sew tassel to top of hat. ■

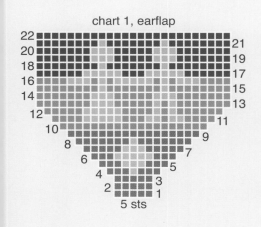

chart 1, earflap

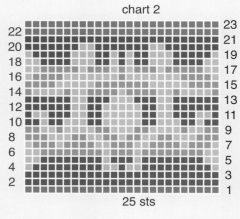

chart 2

25 sts

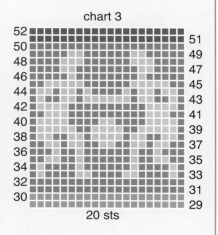

chart 3

20 sts

color key
- ■ Blue (a)
- ■ Green (b)
- ■ Cranberry (c)
- ■ Brown (d)
- ■ Gold (e)

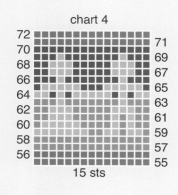

chart 4

15 sts

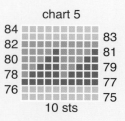

chart 5

10 sts

plaid vest

Yarn
Any DK weight wool blend yarn
- 8¾oz/250g, 670yd/620m (8¾oz/250g, 670yd/620m; 10½oz/300g, 790yd/730m; 10½oz/300g, 790yd/730m) in rainbow (A)
- 5¼oz/150g, 430yd/390m (5¼oz/150g, 430yd/390m; 7oz/200g, 570yd/520m; 7oz/200g, 570yd/520m) of any DK weight cotton/wool blend yarn in beige (B)

Needles
- One pair size 5 (3.75mm) needles *or size to obtain gauge*
- Two size 5 (3.75mm) circular needles, 24"/61cm long

Notions
- Stitch holder

SIZES
Sized for Man's Small (Medium, Large, X-Large). Shown in size Small.

MEASUREMENTS
- **Chest** 42 (44, 46, 48)"/106.5 (111.5, 117, 122)cm.
- **Length** 25½ (26, 27½, 28)"/64.5 (66, 70, 71)cm.

GAUGE
20 sts and 33 rows to 4"/10cm over plaid pat using size 5 (3.75mm) needles.
Take time to check gauge.

NOTES
1 When changing colors, twist yarns on WS to prevent holes in work.
2 Carry color not being used loosely across WS of work.

PLAID PATTERN
(multiple of 5 sts plus 2)
Rows 1 and 3 (RS) With A, k2, *with B, k3, with A, k2; rep from * to end.
Rows 2 and 4 With A, k2, *with B, p3, with A, k2; rep from * to end.
Rows 5–8 With A, knit.
Rep rows 1–8 for plaid pat.

BACK
With A, cast on 107 (112, 117, 122) sts. Knit next 3 rows. Cont in plaid pat and work even until piece measures 15 (15, 16, 16)"/38 (38, 40.5, 40.5)cm from beg, end with row 8.

Shape armhole
Bind off 5 sts at beg of next 2 rows, 4 sts at beg of next 2 rows. Dec 1 st each side on next row, then every other row 3 (4, 4, 4) times more—81 (84, 89, 94) sts. Work even until armhole measures 9½ (10, 10½, 11)"/24 (25.5, 6.5, 28)cm, end with a WS row.

Shape shoulder
Bind off 6 (6, 7, 7) sts at beg of next 6 (4, 8, 4) rows, 7 (7, 0, 8) sts at beg of next 2 (4, 0, 4) rows. Place rem 31 (32, 33, 34) sts on holder for back neck.

FRONT
Work as for back until armhole measures ½ (½, 1, 1½)"/1.5 (1.5, 2.5, 4)cm, end with a WS row.

Shape neck
Next row (RS) Cont to shape armholes, work across to center 3 (2, 3, 2) sts, join a 2nd ball of yarn and bind off center 3 (2, 3, 2) sts, work to end. Working both sides at once, work next row even. Cont to shape armholes, AT THE SAME TIME, dec 1 st from each neck edge on next row, then every 4th row 13 (14, 14, 15) times more. When all shaping is completed, work even on 25 (26, 28, 30) sts each side until piece measures same length as back to shoulder. Shape shoulders as for back.

FINISHING
Block pieces to measurements.
Sew shoulder seams.

Neckband
With RS facing, circular needle and A, pick up and k 55 (58, 58, 60) sts evenly spaced along right neck edge, k31 (32, 33, 34) sts from back neck holder, pick up and k 55 (58, 58, 60) sts evenly spaced along left neck edge—141 (148, 149, 154) sts. Do not join. Work back and forth using 2nd circular needle. Knit next 3 rows. Bind off all sts knitwise. Lap left side edge over right side edge and sew to bound-off sts at beg of neck shaping.

Armhole bands
With RS facing and A, pick up and k 126 (134, 140, 148) sts evenly spaced along armhole edge. Knit next 3 rows. Bind off all sts knitwise. Sew side seams. ■

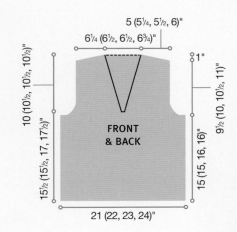

5 (5¼, 5½, 6)"
6¼ (6½, 6½, 6¾)"
10 (10½, 10½, 10½)"
15½ (15½, 17, 17½)"
1"
9½ (10, 10½, 11)"
15 (15, 16, 16)"

FRONT & BACK

21 (22, 23, 24)"

boyfriend hoodie

SIZES
Sized for Man's Small/Medium (Large, X-Large). Shown in sizes Large (on woman) and X-Large (on man).

MEASUREMENTS
• **Chest** 44 (46, 50)"/111.5 (117, 127)cm.
• **Length** 27½ (28½, 29½)"/70 (72.5, 75)cm.
• **Upper arm** 19 (20, 21)"/48 (51, 53)cm.

GAUGE
14 sts and 20 rows to 4"/10cm over St st using larger needles.
Take time to check gauge.

BACK
With smaller needles and CC, cast on 61 (65, 73) sts. Cut this yarn and cont with MC only, work in k1, p1 rib for 4½"/11.5cm, inc 8 sts evenly spaced across last WS row—69 (73, 81) sts.
Change to larger needles and cont in St st, inc 1 st each side every 12th row 4 times—77 (81, 89) sts.
Work even until piece measures 16½ (17, 17½)"/42 (43, 44.5)cm from beg, end with a WS row.

Shape armhole
Bind off 3 sts at beg of next 2 rows. Dec 1 st each side every other row 3 (2, 3) times—65 (71, 77) sts.
Work even until armhole measures 9½ (10, 10½)"/24 (25.5, 26.5)cm, end with a WS row.

Shape neck and shoulders
Bind off 4 (4, 5) sts at beg of next 6 (4, 6) rows, 3 (5, 6) sts at beg of next 2 (4, 2) rows, AT THE SAME TIME, bind off center 19 sts and working both sides at once, bind off 4 sts from each neck edge twice.

LEFT FRONT
With smaller needles and CC, cast on 31 (33, 37) sts. Cut this yarn and cont with MC only, work in k1, p1 rib for 4½"/11.5cm, inc 4 sts evenly spaced across last WS row—35 (37, 41) sts. Change to larger needles.

Pocket
Next row (RS) Work 4 sts, leave rem 31 (33, 37) sts on hold, then turn and cast on 31 (33, 37) sts (for under piece).
Cont in St st on these new sts, working incs as for back, for 40 rows or 8"/20.5cm above rib.
Leave these sts on spare needle and return to 31 (33, 37) sts on hold.
Join yarn and cont in St st on these sts only, dec 1 st at end of each purl row (edge closest to side seam) total of 20 times, end with a WS row—11 (13, 17) sts rem.

Join pocket to front
Next row (RS) Return to under piece sts and beg at side seam, k until 11 (13, 17) sts rem, then holding pocket piece at front with needles parallel, k 1 st from under piece tog with 1 st from pocket on top. Pocket is joined.
Cont in St st on all sts, with incs as on back until piece measures 16½ (17, 17½)"/42 (43, 44.5) cm from beg—39 (41, 45) sts.

Shape armhole
Next row (RS) Bind off 3 sts, work to end. Cont to shape armhole dec 1 st every other row 3 (2, 3) times—33 (36, 39) sts.
Work even until piece measures 23 (24, 25)"/58.5 (61, 63.5) cm from beg, end with a RS row.

Shape neck
Next row (WS) Bind off 4 sts, place a yarn marker (for use in finishing, later), work to end. Cont to shape neck binding off 2 sts from neck edge 7 times more—15 (18, 21) sts.
Work even until armhole measures same as back.

Shape shoulder
Bind off 4 (4, 5) sts from armhole edge 3 (2, 3) times, 3 (5, 6) sts 1 (2, 1) times.

RIGHT FRONT
Work as for left front reversing pocket placement and all shaping.

SLEEVES
With smaller needles and CC, cast on 37 (39, 39) sts. Cut this yarn and cont with MC only, work in k1, p1 rib for 4½"/11.5cm. Change to larger needles and cont in St st inc 1 st each side every 4th row 15 (15, 17) times—67 (69, 73) sts.
Work even until piece measures 19½ (20, 21)"/49.5 (51, 53)cm from beg.

Shape the cap
Bind off 3 sts at beg of next 2 rows, 2 sts at beg of next 8 rows, 3 sts at beg of next 6 rows. Bind off rem 27 (29, 33) sts.

FINISHING
Sew the shoulder seams. Set in sleeves. Sew side and sleeve seams.

Hood
With smaller needles and MC, beg and end at yarn markers on neck (or leaving the 4 bound-off sts at neck edge unworked), pick up and k 81 sts evenly around neck edge. Mark center back neck st. Work in St st for 5 rows.
Inc row (RS) K to marked st, M1, k1, M1, k to end. Rep inc row every 14th row 3 times more—89 sts. Work even until hood measures 11½"/29cm.
Dec row 1 (RS) K43, SK2P and mark this st

Yarn (5)
Any bulky weight acrylic yarn
• 42oz/1190g, 1300yd/1190m (42oz/1190g, 1300yd/1190m; 48oz/1360g, 1480yd/1360m) in dark blue or light blue (MC)
• 6oz/170g, 190yd/180m in light blue or dark blue (CC)

Needles
• One pair each sizes 8 and 10 (5 and 6mm) needles *or size to obtain gauge*
• Spare needle (for 3-needle bind-off)

Notions
• Size G/6 (4.5mm) crochet hook
• One separating zipper, 23 (24, 25)"/58 (60, 64)cm long
• Matching thread and sewing needle
• Stitch holders

boyfriend hoodie

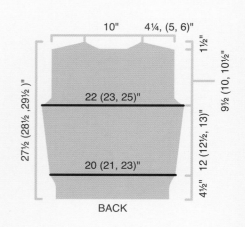

BACK

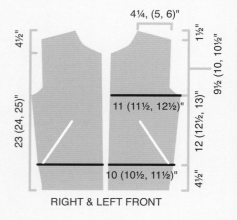

RIGHT & LEFT FRONT

as center, k43—87 sts. Work 1 row even.
Dec row 2 (RS) K to 1 st before marked st, SK2P, k to end. Cont to work SK2P at center of every other row 6 times more—73 sts.
Next row (WS) P35, p2tog, then do not work to end of row. With points of 2 needles tog at center of row and using a 3rd needle, work a 3-needle bind-off as foll: [k1 st of front needle tog with 1 st of back needle] twice, then bind off 1 st. Cont to bind off this way.

Hood trim
With larger needles and MC, pick up and k 99 sts along face edge of hood.
Row 1 (WS) K1, *p1, k1, rep from * to end.
Row 2 (RS) P1, *wyib sl 1, yarn to front and p1; rep from * to end.
Row 3 K1, *wyif sl 1, yarn to back and k1; rep from * to end.
Row 4 (RS) Knit.
Bind off in k1, p1 rib.

Drawstring
With crochet hook, ch for 45"/115cm. Then, using hook, draw chain through elongated knit slip sts on rib trim for drawstring.

Pocket trim
With larger needles and CC, pick up and k 29 sts along shaped pocket edge. Bind off in k1, p1 rib.

Front edge
With larger needles and MC, pick up and k 63 (65, 67) sts along center front edge, including through both thickness to close pocket at center. Bind off in k1, p1 rib. Pin zipper to front opening. Baste and sew zipper in place. Sew bottom of pocket piece to inside of front. ■

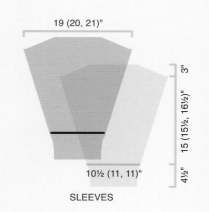

SLEEVES

cabled hat and scarf

Yarn 5
Any bulky weight wool yarn in gray
• 12oz/340g, 420yd/390m for scarf
• 8oz/130g, 180yd/170m for hat

Needles
• One pair size 10 (6mm) needles
  or size to obtain gauge

Notions
• Cable needle (cn)

SIZE
One size.

MEASUREMENTS
• **Scarf** 6 × 75"/15.5 × 190.5cm.
• **Hat Circumference** Approx 20"/51cm slightly stretched.

GAUGES
• 24 sts and 19 rows to 4"/10cm over cable pat for scarf using size 10 (6mm) needles.
• 18 sts and 21 rows to 4"/10cm over cable pat for hat using size 10 (6mm) needles.
Take time to check gauges.

STITCH GLOSSARY
4-st RC Sl 2 sts to cn and hold to *back*, k2, k2 from cn.
4-st LC Sl 2 sts to cn and hold to *front*, k2, k2 from cn.
6-st RC Sl 3 sts to cn and hold to *back*, k3, k3 from cn.
6-st LC Sl 3 sts to cn and hold to *front*, k3, k3 from cn.

SCARF CABLE PATTERN
(over 36 sts)
Rows 1 and 5 (RS) [P2, 4-st LC, p2, k6] twice, p2, 4-st LC, p2.
Rows 2, 4 and 6 K the knit sts and p the purl sts.
Row 3 [P2, 4-st LC, p2, 6-st LC] twice, p2, 4-st LC, p2. Rep rows 1–6 for scarf cable pat.

HAT CABLE PATTERN
(multiple of 18 sts)
Rows 1 and 5 *P2, 4-st RC, p4, k6, p2; rep from * to end.
Rows 2, 4 and 6 K the knit sts and p the purl sts.
Row 3 *P2, 4-st RC, p4, 6-st RC, p2; rep from * to end.
Rep rows 1–6 for hat cable pat.

SCARF
Cast on 36 sts. Work in scarf cable pat until piece measures 75"/190.5cm from beg. Bind off in pat.

HAT
Cast on 90 sts.

Brim
Work rows 1–6 of hat cable pat (working 18-st rep 5 times) for 17 rows—piece measures approx 3¼"/8cm from beg. K 1 row on WS for turning ridge.
Note The next row will be a RS row of the crown, but the WS of the brim. Brim will be folded up later.

Crown
Beg with row 1 (RS) of pat, cont in hat cable pat until piece measures 8"/20.5cm from beg, end with a WS row.

Shape top
Cont in cable pat, working decs as foll:
Dec row 1 (RS) P2, [work 4 sts, p1, p2tog, p1, work 6 sts, p1, p2tog, p1] 4 times, work 4 sts, p1, p2tog, p1, work 6 sts, p2—81 sts. Work 1 row even.
Dec row 2 (RS) P2, [work 4 sts, p1, p2tog, work 6 sts, p1, p2tog] 4 times, work 4 sts, p1, p2tog, work 6 sts, p2—72 sts. Work 1 row even.
Dec row 3 (RS) P2tog, [work 4 sts, p2tog, work 6 sts, p2tog] 4 times, work 4 sts, p2tog, work 6 sts, p2tog—61 sts. Work 1 row even.
Dec row 4 (RS) [P1, k1, k2tog, p2tog, work 6 sts] 5 times, p1—51 sts. Work 1 row even.
Dec row 5 (RS) [K2tog twice, work 6 sts] 5 times, p1—41 sts. Work 1 row even.
Dec row 6 (RS) [K2tog twice, work 4 sts] 5 times, p1—31 sts. Cut yarn, leaving a 12"/30.5cm end for sewing. Draw yarn through rem sts, gather tog tightly and sew back seam. ■

Shannon Geer for Iварepresents.com

zippered jacket

Yarn (5)
- 35oz/980g, 1080yd/990m (40oz/1120g, 1230yd/1130m; 45oz/1260g, 1380yd/1270m; 50oz/1400g, 1530yd/1400m) of any bulky weight wool and acrylic blend yarn in orange

Needles
- One pair each sizes 9 and 10½ (5.5 and 6.5mm) needles *or size to obtain gauge*

Notions
- Heavy duty separating zipper, 26 (26, 28, 28)"/66 (66, 70, 70)cm long
- Matching thread and sewing needle
- Stitch holders
- Stitch markers

SIZES
Sized for Man's Small (Medium, Large, X-Large). Shown in size Medium.

MEASUREMENTS
- **Chest** 45 (48, 52, 56)"/114 (122, 132, 142)cm.
- **Length** 26¾ (26¾, 28¾, 28¾)"/68 (68, 73, 73)cm.
- **Upper arm** 19 (20, 21, 22)"/48 (51, 53, 56)cm.

GAUGE
13 sts and 18 rows to 4"/10cm over St st using larger needles.
Take time to check gauge.

FARROW RIB PATTERN
(multiple of 3 sts plus 1)
Row 1 (WS) P1, * k2, p1; rep from * to end.
Row 2 * K2, p1; rep from * end k1. Rep these 2 rows for farrow rib pat.

BACK
With smaller needles, cast on 73 (79, 85, 91) sts. Beg with a WS row, work in farrow rib pat for a total of 13 rows.
Change to larger needles and cont in St st until piece measures 17¼ (16¾, 18¼, 17¾)"/44 (42.5, 46.5, 45)cm from beg, end with a WS row.

Paul Amato

Shape armhole

Bind off 8 (9, 10, 11) sts at beg of next 2 rows—57 (61, 65, 69) sts.
Work even until armhole measures 7½ (8, 8½, 9)"/19 (20.5, 21.5, 23)cm.
Bind off loosely.

LEFT FRONT

With smaller needles, cast on 39 (42, 45, 48) sts.
Row 1 (WS) K2 (garter st edge), pm, work in farrow rib pat to end.
Keeping the 2 center front sts in garter st, work in farrow rib pat on rem sts for a total of 13 rows.
Change to larger needles and keeping 2 garter sts, cont in St st on rem sts until piece measures same as back to armhole, end with a WS row.

Shape armhole

Next row (RS) Bind off 8 (9, 10, 11) sts, work to end—31 (33, 35, 37) sts.
Work even until armhole measures 6½ (7, 7½, 8)"/16.5 (18, 19, 20.5)cm, end with a RS row.

Shape neck

Next row (WS) Work first 8 (8, 9, 9) sts and sl to a holder, work to end.
Cont to shape neck, binding off 3 sts from neck edge every other row twice—17 (19, 20, 22) sts.
Bind off rem sts for shoulder.

RIGHT FRONT

Work as for left front, reversing placement of front band and all shaping.

LEFT SLEEVE

With smaller needles, cast on 40 (40, 46, 46) sts. Beg with a WS row, work in farrow rib pat for a total of 13 rows.
Change to larger needles.
Next row (RS) Work in St st across 12 (12, 15, 15) sts, pm, cont in farrow rib pat across next 16 sts, pm, work rem 12 (12, 15, 15) sts in St st.
Cont to work in this way for 3 rows more.

Inc row (RS) K1, inc 1 st in next st, k to last 2 sts, inc 1 st in next st, k1. Rep inc row (working increased sts in St st) every 4th row 1 (9, 2, 4) times more, every 6th row 11 (6, 11, 10) times—66 (72, 74, 76) sts.
Work even until piece measures 22 (22½, 23, 23¾)"/56 (57, 58.5, 60) cm from beg, end with a WS row.

Shape cap

Bind off 24 (27, 28, 29) sts at beg of next 2 rows.

Make saddle shoulder

Cont in farrow rib pat on the rem 18 sts (the k 1 st each side of pat sts will be a selvage st for seaming later) for 5¼ (6, 6¼, 6¾)"/13.5 (15, 16, 17)cm, end with a RS row.

Shape neck edge

Next row (WS) Bind off 8 sts (front neck edge) work to end. Dec 1 st at neck edge every row 4 times—6 sts. Work even for 10 (10, 12, 12) rows more in pat.
Bind off all sts loosely.

RIGHT SLEEVE

Work as for left sleeve, reversing the neck edge shaping (with the bind-offs and de-creases at beg of RS rows).

FINISHING

Block pieces to measurements.
Set in sleeves, sewing the saddle shoulder across the top of the front and back shoulders.
Join 6-st strip at the center back neck.
Sew side and sleeve seams.

Collar

With smaller needles, work in pat across 8 (8, 9, 9) sts from right front neck holder, pick up and k 55 (55, 59, 59) sts evenly around neck edge, work in pat across the 8 (8, 9, 9) sts from left front neck hold-ers—71 (71, 77, 77) sts.
Work in farrow rib pat (with k2

sts at each end) for 3"/7.5cm.
Bind off loosely in pat.

Sew in zipper

Pin or baste zipper in place along the front edge.
Sew zipper in place. ■

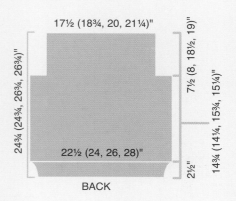

17½ (18¾, 20, 21¼)"
24¾ (24¾, 26¾, 26¾)"
7½ (8, 18½, 19)"
14¾ (14¼, 15¾, 15¼)"
22½ (24, 26, 28)"
2½"

BACK

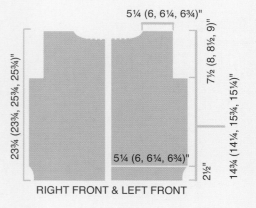

5¼ (6, 6¼, 6¾)"
23¾ (23¾, 25¾, 25¾)"
7½ (8, 8½, 9)"
14¾ (14¼, 15¾, 15¼)"
5¼ (6, 6¼, 6¾)"
2½"

RIGHT FRONT & LEFT FRONT

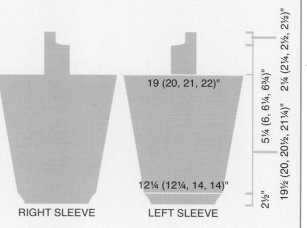

19 (20, 21, 22)"
2¼ (2¼, 2½, 2½)"
5¼ (6, 6¼, 6¾)"
19½ (20, 20½, 21¼)"
12¼ (12¼, 14, 14)"
2½"

RIGHT SLEEVE   LEFT SLEEVE

preppy cabled vest

SIZES
Sized for Man's Small (Medium, Large).
Shown in size Small.

MEASUREMENTS
• **Chest** 40 (45, 50)"/101.5 (114, 127)cm.
• **Length** 25 (25½, 26½)"/63.5 (65, 67)cm.

GAUGES
• 18 sts and 26 rows to 4"/10cm over St st using size 7 (4.5mm) needles.
• 21 sts and 26 rows to 4"/10cm over cable pat foll chart using size 7 (4.5mm) needles.
Take time to check gauges.

K2, P2 RIB
(multiple of 4 sts)
Row 1 (RS) P1, *k2, p2; rep from *, end k2, p1.
Row 2 K1, *p2, k2; rep from *, end p2, k1.
Rep rows 1 and 2 for k2, p2 rib.

STITCH GLOSSARY
9-stitch left cable (9-st lc)
SI 5 sts to cn and hold to front of work, k4; then k5 from cn.

BACK
With MC, cast on 96 (108, 120) sts. Work in k2, p2 rib for 3½"/9cm. Work in St st in stripes as foll: 8 rows each A, B and C (24 rows in total), and inc 9 (11, 11) sts evenly across the last C row—105 (119, 131) sts. Change to MC.

Yarn [4]
• 15oz/420g, 710yd/650m (15oz/420g, 710yd/650m; 20oz/560g, 950yd/870m) of any worsted weight cotton yarn each in cream (MC), medium blue (A), light yellow (B) and navy (C)

Needles
• One pair size 7 (4.5mm) needles, *or size to obtain gauge*
• Size 7 (4.5mm) circular needle, 24"/60cm long

Notions
• Cable needle (cn)
• Stitch holders

Beg chart
Row 1 (RS) Beg as indicated for size, work to rep line, work the 17-st rep 5 (6, 7) times, ending last rep as indicated. Cont in pat as established until 16 rows of chart have been worked 3 times, then work rows 1–14 (1–14, 1–16) once more—piece measures approx 16½ (16½, 17)"/42 (42, 43)cm from beg, end with a WS row.

Shape armholes
Bind off 3 sts at beg of next 8 (10, 10) rows, then 2 sts at beg of next 0 (0, 2) rows—81 (89, 97) sts. Work evenly in chart pat until armhole measures 8½ (9, 9½)"/21 (23, 24)cm. Bind off.

FRONT
Work same as back to armhole.

Shape armholes and v-neck
Work armhole decreases same as back, AT THE SAME TIME, bind off center st for neck and working both sides at once, dec 1 sts at each neck edge (working k2tog) every other row 23 (23, 25) times—17 (21, 23) sts each side. Work even until same length as back. Bind off rem sts each side for shoulders.

Left front striped neckband
With RS facing and A, beg at left front shoulder edge, pick up and k 43 (45, 47) sts evenly along left front V-neck edge, ending at center front. Work in St st and stripes as foll: 5 rows A, 6 rows B, 6 rows C, AT THE SAME TIME, dec 1 st at center front edge every other row. Place rem sts on a holder. Work in same way along right front neck edge.

FINISHING
Sew shoulder seams, sewing sides of striped neckband along back shoulder edge.

Ribbed neckband
With RS facing and MC, work sts from left front, pm, then work sts from right front holder, pick up and k 32 (32, 36) sts evenly along back neck. Join and work in k2, p2 rib as foll:
Rnd 1 *K2, p2; rep from * to 2 sts before

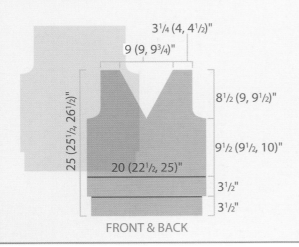

FRONT & BACK

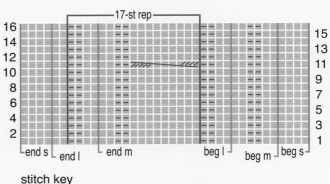

stitch key
▨ k on rs, p on ws
▬ p on rs, k on ws
▨▨▨▨ 9-st lpc

marker, k2tog, sl marker, k2tog, beg with k
or p (so that rnd will end with a p2), work
in k2, p2 rib to end.
Rep last rnd 4 times more. Bind off in rib.

Armhole band
With RS facing and MC, pick up and k 92
(96, 100) sts evenly around each armhole
edge. Work in k2, p2 rib for 5 rows. Bind off
in rib. Sew side and armhole band seams. ■

Rose Callahan

zippered cardigan

SIZES
Sized for Man's Small (Medium, Large, X-Large). Shown in size Medium.

MEASUREMENTS
- **Chest (closed)** 42 (46, 49½, 54)"/106.5 (117, 125.5, 137)cm.
- **Length** 26½ (27, 27½, 28)"/67.5 (68.5, 70, 71)cm.
- **Upper arm** 20 (21, 21¾, 22¾)"/51 (53.5, 55, 57.5)cm.

GAUGE
17 sts and 22 rows to 4"/10cm over St st using larger needles.
Take time to check gauge.

SLIP STITCH PATTERN
(multiple of 4 sts plus 3)
Row 1 (RS) With MC, knit.
Row 2 With MC, purl.
Row 3 With A, k3, *sl 1 wyib, k3; rep from * to end.
Row 4 With A, p3, *sl 1 wyif, p3; rep from * to end.
Row 5 With B, k1, *sl 1 wyib, k3; rep from *, end sl 1 wyib, k1.
Row 6 With B, k1, *sl 1 wyif, k3; rep from *, end sl 1 wyif, k1.
Row 7 With A, rep row 3.
Row 8 With A, rep row 4.
Row 9 With MC, k1, *sl 1 wyib, k3; rep from *, end sl 1 wyib, k1.
Row 10 With MC, p1, *sl 1 wyif, p3; rep from *, end sl 1 wyif, p1.
Rep rows 1–10 for slip st pat.

BACK
With smaller needles and MC, cast on 89 (97, 105, 115) sts. Work in k1, p1 rib for 2½"/6.5cm, end with a WS row. Change to larger needles and work in St st until piece measures 16½"/42cm from beg, end with a WS row.

Yarn (4)
Any worsted weight wool yarn
- 15¾oz/450g, 990yd/910m (15¾oz/450g, 990yd/910m; 17½oz/500g, 1090yd/1000m; 19¼oz/550g, 1200yd/1100m) in teal (MC)
- 1¾oz/50g, 110yd/100m each in royal blue (A) and light olive (B)

Needles
- One pair each sizes 7 and 8 (4.5 and 5mm) needles *or size to obtain gauge*

Notions
- One 26 (26, 27, 27)"/66 (66, 68.5, 68.5)cm separating zipper

Armhole shaping
Bind off 4 sts at beg of next 2 rows, 3 sts at beg of next 2 rows, then dec 1 st at each side every other row once—73 (81, 89, 99) sts. Work even until armhole measures 10 (10½, 11, 11½)"/25.5 (26.5, 28, 29)cm, end with a WS row. Bind off.

LEFT FRONT
With smaller needles and MC, cast on 43 (47, 51, 55) sts. Work in k1, p1 rib for 2½"/6.5cm, end with a WS row. Change to larger needles and work in sl st pat until piece measures 16½"/42cm from beg, end with a WS row.

Armhole shaping
Next row (RS) Bind off 4 sts, work to end. Cont to shape armhole, binding off 3 sts from armhole edge once, dec 1 st every other row once—35 (39, 43, 47) sts. Work even until armhole measures 7½ (7½, 8½, 8½)"/19 (19, 21.5, 21.5)cm, end with a RS row.

Neck shaping
Next row (WS) Bind off 8 sts, work to end. Cont to shape neck edge, binding off 4 sts once, 3 sts once, dec 1 st every other row once—19 (23, 27, 31) sts. Work even until piece measures same length as back to shoulder, end with a WS row. Bind off.

RIGHT FRONT
Work as for left front, reversing all shaping.

SLEEVES
With smaller needles and MC, cast on 41 (43, 45, 45) sts. Work in k1, p1 rib for 2½"/6.5cm, inc 0 (2, 2, 4) sts evenly spaced across last row—41 (45, 47, 49) sts. Change to larger needles and St st. Inc 1 st each side on next row, then every 4th row 21 (21, 22, 23) times more—85 (89, 93, 97) sts. Work even until piece measures 19 (19, 19½, 20)"/48 (48, 49.5, 51)cm from beg, end with a WS row.

Cap shaping
Bind off 4 sts at beg of next 2 rows, 3 sts at beg of next 2 rows, then dec 1 st at each side every other row 8 times. Bind off rem 55 (59, 63, 67) sts.

FINISHING
Lightly block pieces to measurements. Sew shoulder seams.

Front bands
With RS facing, smaller needles and MC, pick up and k 113 (115, 117, 119) sts evenly spaced along left front edge. Work in k1, p1 rib for 2 rows. Bind off loosely in rib. Rep for right front edge.

Collar
With RS facing, smaller needles and MC, pick up and k 85 (85, 85, 87) sts evenly spaced along entire neck edge. Work in k1, p1 rib for 2"/5cm. Bind off loosely in rib. Set in sleeves. Sew side and sleeve seams. Sew in zipper. ■

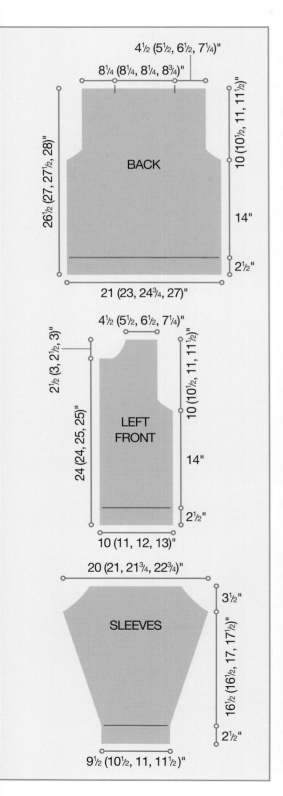

BACK

4½ (5½, 6½, 7¼)"

8¼ (8¼, 8¼, 8¾)"

26½ (27, 27½, 28)"

10 (10½, 11, 11½)"

14"

2½"

21 (23, 24¾, 27)"

LEFT FRONT

4½ (5½, 6½, 7¼)"

2½ (3, 2½, 3)"

24 (24, 25, 25)"

10 (10½, 11, 11½)"

14"

2½"

10 (11, 12, 13)"

SLEEVES

20 (21, 21¾, 22¾)"

3½"

16½ (16½, 17, 17½)"

2½"

9½ (10½, 11, 11½)"

jolly roger sweater

Yarn 6

Any super bulky weight wool and acrylic blend yarn
- 36oz/1020g, 640yd/590m (42oz/1190g, 750yd/690m; 48oz/1360g, 850yd/690m) in black
- 6oz/170g, 106yd/97m in cream

Needles
- One pair each sizes 11 and 13 (8mm and 9mm) needles or size to obtain gauge

Notions
- Stitch holder

SIZES
Sized for unisex sizes Small (Medium, Large). Shown in size Small.

MEASUREMENTS
- **Chest/Bust** 35½ (37, 39)"/90 (94, 99)cm.
- **Length** 25½ (26, 26½)"/65 (66, 67)cm.
- **Upper arm** 17 (18, 18½)"/43 (45.5, 47)cm.

GAUGE
9 sts and 11 rows to 4"/10cm over St st using larger needles.
Take time to check gauge.

NOTES
1 Make the front first.
2 Chart may be worked using bobbins for the separate blocks of color or stranding color not in use loosely at back of work.

FRONT
With smaller needles and black, cast on 40 (42, 44) sts. Work in k2, p2 rib for 6 rows. Change to larger needles and cont in St st until piece measures 9 (9½, 10)"/23 (24, 25.5)cm from beg, end with a WS row.

Beg chart
Row 1 (RS) With black k6 (7, 8), work row 1 of the 28-st chart, with black k6 (7, 8). Cont to foll chart in this way, through row

27, AT THE SAME TIME, when piece measures 16"/40.5cm from beg, end with a WS row, work as foll:

Shape armhole
Bind off 2 sts at beg of next 2 rows.
Next (dec) row (RS) K1, ssk, k to last 3 sts, k2tog, k1—34 (36, 38) sts. Work even until armhole measures 5½ (6, 6½)"/14 (15, 16.5) cm.

Shape neck
Next row (RS) K10 (11, 12), k2tog, sl the center 10 sts to st holder, join a 2nd ball of yarn and k2tog, k10 (11, 12). Working both

sides at once with separate balls of yarn, dec 1 st at each neck edge every other row 5 times more. Bind off rem 6 (7, 8) sts each side for shoulders.

BACK
Make same as for front, without chart pat, until armhole measures 9½ (10, 10½)"/24 (25.5, 26.5)cm, end with a WS row.

Shape shoulder
Bind off 6 (7, 8) sts, k22 and sl these sts to a holder, bind off rem 6 (7, 8) sts.

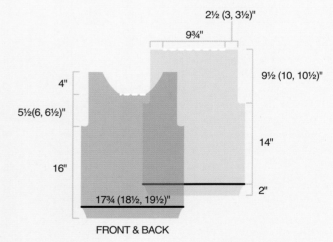

2½ (3, 3½)"
9¾"
9½ (10, 10½)"
4"
5½(6, 6½)"
14"
16"
2"
17¾ (18½, 19½)"

FRONT & BACK

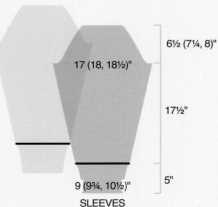

6½ (7¼, 8)"
17 (18, 18½)"
17½"
9 (9¾, 10½)"
5"

SLEEVES

SLEEVES

With smaller needles and black, cast on
20 (22, 24) sts. Work in k1, p1 rib for 16
rows. Change to larger needles. Cont in
St st, inc 1 st each side every 4th row 5
times, every 6th row 4 times—38 (40,
42) sts. Work even until piece measures
22½"/57 cm from beg.

Shape cap
Bind off 2 sts at beg of next 2 rows.
Next (dec) row (RS) K1, ssk, k to last 3
sts, k2tog, k1. Rep dec row every other
row 8 (9, 10) times more. Bind off rem
16 sts.

TURTLENECK

Sew left shoulder seam. With smaller
needles and black, work in k1, p1 rib
across 22 sts from back neck holder, pick
up and k 8 sts along side of front neck,
work in k1, p1 rib across 10 sts from
front neck holder, pick up and k 8 sts
along side of front neck—48 sts. Work in
k1, p1 rib for 7"/18cm. Bind off in rib.

FINISHING

Sew right shoulder and turtleneck seam,
sewing top half of collar for seam to
show on RS for collar foldback. Set in
sleeves. Sew side and sleeve seams. ■

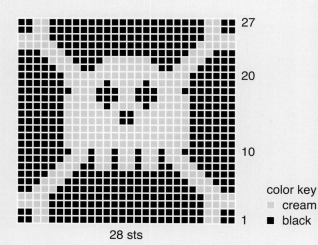

27

20

10

1

28 sts

color key
cream
black

Haitem

men's polo

Yarn (4)
• 21oz/600g, 830yd/760m (24½oz/700g, 970yd/890m; 28oz/800g, 1110yd/1020m; 31½oz/900g, 1250yd/1150m; 35oz/1000g, 1380yd/1270m) of any worsted weight wool yarn in navy

Needles
• One pair each sizes 8 and 9 (5 and 5.5mm) needles *or size to obtain gauge*
• Size 8 (5mm) circular needle, 16"/40cm long

Notions
• Stitch markers

SIZES
Sized for Men's Small (Medium, Large, 1X, 2X).

MEASUREMENTS
• **Chest** 38 (42, 46, 50, 54)"/96.5 (106.5, 117, 127, 137)cm.
• **Length** 24½ (25, 26, 26½, 27½)"/62 (63.5, 66, 67.5, 70)cm.
• **Upper arm** 17 (18, 19, 20, 21)"/43 (45.5, 48, 51, 53.5)cm.

GAUGE
17 sts and 24 rows to 4"/10cm over St st using larger needles.
Take time to check gauge.

K3, P3 RIB
(multiple of 6 sts plus 2)
Row 1 (WS) K1 (selvage st), *p3, k3; rep from * to last st, k1 (selvage st).
Row 2 K1, *p3, k3; rep from * to last st, k1. Rep rows 1 and 2 for k3, p3 rib.

BACK
With smaller needles, cast on 80 (92, 98, 104, 116) sts. Work in k3, p3 rib for 11 rows. Change to larger needles, and work in St st (k on RS, p on WS) until piece

measures 15 (15, 15½, 15½, 16)"/38 (38, 39.5, 39.5, 40.5)cm from beg, end with a WS row.

Shape armhole
Bind off 8 (9, 10, 12, 13) sts at beg of next 2 rows—64 (74, 78, 80, 90) sts. Work even until armhole measures 8½ (9, 9½, 10, 10½)"/21.5 (23, 24, 25.5, 26.5)cm, end with a WS row.

Shape shoulder
Bind off 6 (7, 8, 8, 9) sts at beg of next 4 rows, 5 (7, 6, 6, 8) sts at beg of next 2 rows. Bind off rem 30 (32, 34, 36, 38) sts for back neck.

FRONT
Work as for the back until armhole measures 1½ (2, 2½, 3, 3½)"/4 (5, 6.5, 7.5, 9)cm, end with a WS row.

Shape placket
Next row (RS) K28 (33, 35, 36, 41), join 2nd ball of yarn and bind off center 8 sts, k to end. Working both sides at once with separate balls of yarn, work even for 5"/12.5cm.

Shape neck and shoulder
Bind off from each neck edge 3 (4, 5, 6, 7) sts once, 2 sts twice, then dec 1 st from each neck edge every other row 4 times—17 (21, 22, 22, 26) sts each side. Work even until armhole measures 8½ (9, 9½, 10, 10½)"/21.5 (23, 24, 25.5, 26.5)cm. Shape shoulder as for the back.

SLEEVES
With smaller needles, cast on 38 (38, 38, 44, 44) sts. Work in k3, p3 rib for 11 rows as for back. Change to larger needles, St st and work 4 rows even in St st.
Inc row (RS) K1, M1, k to last st, M1, k1. Work inc row every 4th row 1 (7, 13, 13, 19) times more, then every 6th row 15 (11, 7, 7, 3) times—72 (76, 80, 86, 90) sts. Work even until piece measures 20 (20, 20¼, 19¾, 20)"/51 (51, 51.5, 50, 51)cm from beg.

Place stitch markers at beg and end of row. Work even for 2 (2, 2¼, 2¾, 3)"/5 (5, 5.5, 7, 7.5)cm more. Bind off.

FINISHING
Sew shoulder seams.

Right front placket
With smaller needles and RS facing, pick up and k 23 sts.
Row 1 (WS) K1, *p3, k3; rep from * to last 4 sts, end p3, k1.
Row 2 K1, *k3, p3; rep from * to last 4 sts, end k4.
Rep rows 1 and 2 until placket measures 1¾"/4.5cm. Bind off in rib.

Left front placket
Work to correspond to right front placket.

Collar
With circular needle and RS facing, pick up and k 20 (21, 22, 23, 24) sts along right front neck, 29 (30, 34, 35, 39) sts along back, 20 (21, 22, 23, 24) sts along left front neck—69 (72, 78, 81, 87) sts.
Row 1 (RS) K3 (garter border), *k3, p3; rep from * to last 6 sts, end k6 (3 sts for rib, 3 sts for garter border).
Row 2 K3, *p3, k3; rep from * to last 6 sts, p3, k3.
Rep rows 1 and 2 until collar measures 4½"/11.5cm. Bind off in rib.
Set in sleeves, sewing 2 (2, 2¼, 2¾, 3)"/5 (5, 5.5, 7, 7.5)cm at top of sleeve above markers to bound-off armhole sts. Sew ends of right and left plackets to center bound-off placket sts on front. Sew side and sleeve seams. ■

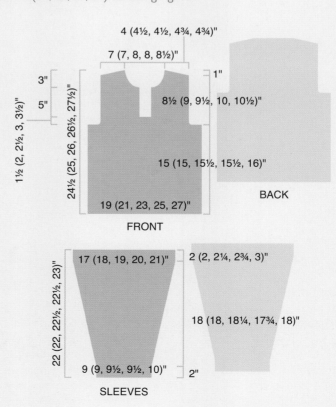

4 (4½, 4½, 4¾, 4¾)"

7 (7, 8, 8, 8½)"

3"

5"

8½ (9, 9½, 10, 10½)"

1"

1½ (2, 2½, 3, 3½)"

24½ (25, 26, 26½, 27½)"

15 (15, 15½, 15½, 16)"

BACK

19 (21, 23, 25, 27)"

FRONT

17 (18, 19, 20, 21)"

2 (2, 2¼, 2¾, 3)"

22 (22, 22½, 22½, 23)"

18 (18, 18¼, 17¾, 18)"

9 (9, 9½, 9½, 10)"

2"

SLEEVES

39

zippered vest

SIZES
Sized for Man's Small, Medium, Large, X-Large. Shown in size Medium.

MEASUREMENTS
- **Chest** 45½ (49, 52½, 56)"/115.5 (124.5, 133, 142)cm.
- **Length** 26½ (27, 28, 28½)"/67 (68.5, 71, 72.5)cm.

GAUGE
18 sts and 24 rows to 4"/10cm over St st using size 8 (5mm) needles.
Take time to check gauge.

BACK
With MC, cast on 94 (102, 110, 118) sts. Work in k2, p2 rib as foll:
Row 1 (RS) K2, *p2, k2; rep from * to end.
Row 2 P2, *k2, p2; rep from * to end.
Rep rows 1 and 2 until piece measures 3"/7.5cm from beg, end with a WS row. Change to CC and k 1 row, p 1 row. Change to MC and work 16 rows in St st (k on RS, p on WS). Inc 1 st at each side on next row, then every 14th row 3 times more—102 (110, 118, 126) sts. Work even until piece measures 16 (16, 16½, 16½)"/40.5 (40.5, 42, 42)cm from beg, end with a WS row.

Shape armhole
Bind off 4 (4, 5, 5) sts at beg of next 2 rows, 3 sts at beg of next 2 rows, 2 sts at beg of next 4 (4, 6, 6) rows. Dec 1 st at each side every other row 2 (3, 2, 4) times—76 (82, 86, 90) sts. Work even until armhole measures 8½ (9, 9½, 10)"/21.5 (23, 24, 25.5)cm, end with a WS row.

Shape shoulder and neck
Bind off 3 (3, 5, 5) sts at beg of next 6 (2, 2, 4) rows, 4 sts at beg of next 6 (10, 10, 8) rows, AT THE SAME TIME, after 4 rows of shoulder shaping have been worked, bind off center 18 (20, 20, 22) sts for neck, and working both sides at once, bind off 3 sts from neck edge twice and 2 sts once.

FRONT
Work as for back until piece measures 16 (16, 16½, 16½)"/40.5 (40.5, 42, 42)cm from beg, end with a WS row.

Shape armhole and neck
Shape armholes same as back, AT THE SAME TIME, when armhole measures 1½ (2, 2½, 3)"/4 (5, 6.5, 7.5)cm, mark center of row, and work as foll:
Next row (RS) K to 2 sts before marker, join CC and k4, join new ball of MC and work to end. Working both sides at once, work 3 more rows in St st, matching colors and cont to shape armhole.

Shape placket
Next row (RS) Work in colors as established to center, join 2nd ball of CC and work in colors as established to end. Working both sides at once, work even, keeping 2 neck edge sts each side in CC and all other sts in MC, until armhole measures 7½ (8, 8½, 9)"/19 (20.5, 21.5, 23)cm.

Shape neck and shoulder
Bind off from each neck edge 4 (5, 5, 6) sts once, 4 sts once, 3 sts once, 2 sts once, dec 1 st every other row 4 times. AT THE SAME TIME, when armhole measures same as back to shoulder, shape shoulder at side edge same as back.

FINISHING
Block pieces to measurements. Sew shoulder seams.

Collar
With RS facing and CC, pick up and k 26 (27, 27, 28) sts along right front neck, 42 (44, 44, 46) sts along back neck, and 26 (27, 27, 28) sts along left front neck—94 (98, 98, 102) sts. P 1 row.
Next row (RS) With CC, k2, with MC, k to last 2 sts, with CC, k2.
Next row With CC, p2, with MC, p2, *k2, p2; rep from * to last 2 sts, with CC, p2.
Next row With CC, k2, with MC, k2, *p2, k2; rep from * to last 2 sts, with CC, k2.
Rep last 2 rows 8 times more, then rep row 2 once more.
Cut MC. With CC, k 1 row, p 1 row, then bind off all sts.
Sew side seams.

Crochet trim
With RS facing, CC and crochet hook, work 1 rnd sc evenly around each armhole edge. Work 1 row sl st into armhole, working from the underarm up to the shoulder, just inside single crochet edging.
With CC, work 2 adjacent rows of sl st along shoulder seams, working from the outside in.
Sew zipper into placket and collar edge. ■

Yarn 4
Any worsted weight wool yarn
- 17½oz/500g, 690yd/630m (17½oz/500g, 690yd/630m; 21oz/600g, 830yd/760m; 24½oz/700g, 970yd/890m) in brown (MC)
- 3½oz/100g, 140yd/130m in green (CC)

Needles
- One pair size 8 (5mm) needles *or size to obtain gauge*

Notions
- Size I/9 (5.5mm) crochet hook
- One 10"/25cm zipper
- Stitch holder and markers
- Sewing needle and thread

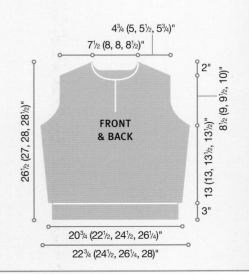

4¾ (5, 5½, 5¾)"

7½ (8, 8, 8½)"

2"

8½ (9, 9½, 10)"

FRONT & BACK

26½ (27, 28, 28½)"

13 (13, 13½, 13½)"

3"

20¾ (22½, 24½, 26¼)"

22¾ (24½, 26¼, 28)"

rollneck sweater

SIZES
Sized for Man's X-Small (Small, Medium, Large, X-Large). Shown in size Small.

MEASUREMENTS
- **Chest** 40 (44, 48, 52, 56)"/101.5 (112, 123, 132, 142)cm.
- **Length** 24½ (25, 25½, 26, 26½)"/62 (63.5, 64.5, 66, 67)cm.
- **Upper arm** 17 (17¾, 18¾, 19½, 20½)"/43 (45, 47.5, 59.5, 52)cm.

GAUGE
18 sts and 26 rows to 4"/10cm over St st using size 7 (4.5mm) needles.
Take time to check gauge.

BACK
Cast on 90 (100, 108, 118, 126) sts. Work in St st for 16"/40.5cm, end with a WS row.

30

Shape armhole
Bind off 0 (0, 0, 4, 5) sts at beg of next 2 rows.
Next (dec) row (RS) K6, ssk, k to last 8 sts, k2tog, k6.
Work dec row every other row 4 (6, 9, 9, 11) times more—80 (86, 88, 90, 92) sts.
Work even until armhole measures 7½ (8, 8½, 9, 9½)"/19 (20.5, 21.5, 23, 24)cm, end with a WS row.

Shape shoulder and neck
Bind off 7 (8, 8, 9, 9) sts at beg of next 4 rows, 8 (9, 9, 8, 8) sts at beg of next 2 rows, AT THE SAME TIME, bind off center 32 (32, 34, 34, 36) sts and working both sides at same time, bind off 2 sts from each neck edge once.

FRONT
Work as for back until armhole measures 6½ (7, 7½, 8, 8½)"/16.5 (18, 19, 20.5, 21.5) cm, end with a WS row.

Shape neck and shoulder
Next row (RS) Work 27 (30, 30, 31, 31) sts, join 2nd ball of yarn and bind off center 26

Yarn ④
- 15¾oz/450g, 990yd/910m (17½oz/500g, 1110yd/1020m; 19¼oz/550g, 1210yd/1110m; 21oz/600g, 1320yd/1210m; 22¾oz/650g, 1430yd/1310m) of any worsted weight wool yarn in self-striping brown, green and blue

Needles
- One pair size 7 (4.5mm) needles *or size to obtain gauge*

(26, 28, 28, 30) sts, work to end. Working both sides at same time with separate balls of yarn, shape neck and shoulders as foll:
Next (dec) row K to last 8 sts on first side, k2tog, k6; on 2nd side, k6, ssk, k to end. Work dec row every other row 4 times more, AT THE SAME TIME, when same length as back to shoulder, shape shoulder as for back.

SLEEVES
Cast on 46 (46, 46, 50, 50) sts. Work even in St st for 6 rows.

Next (inc) row (RS) K1, M1, k to last st, M1, k1.
Work inc row every 6th row 0 (5, 11, 11, 18) times and every 8th row 14 (11, 7, 7, 2) times—76 (80, 84, 88, 92) sts. Work until piece measures 20¾ (20¾, 21½, 21¼, 21¾)"/52.5 (52.5, 54, 54, 55)cm from beg.

Shape sleeve cap
Bind off 3 sts at beg of next 8 rows. Bind off rem 52 (56, 60, 64, 68) sts.

FINISHING
Sew left shoulder seam.

Work neckband
Beg at right front, with RS facing pick up and k 40 (40, 42, 42, 44) sts along front neck, 38 (38, 40, 40, 42) sts along back neck—78 (78, 82, 82, 86) sts. Work in St st for 10 rows. Bind off loosely.
Sew right shoulder and neckband seam, switching seam to RS at curl.
Set in sleeves. Sew side and sleeve seams. ■

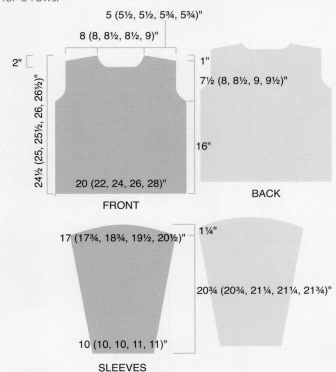

5 (5½, 5½, 5¾, 5¾)"

8 (8, 8½, 8½, 9)"

2"

24½ (25, 25½, 26, 26½)"

20 (22, 24, 26, 28)"

FRONT

1"

7½ (8, 8½, 9, 9½)"

16"

BACK

17 (17¾, 18¾, 19½, 20½)"

1¼"

20¾ (20¾, 21¼, 21¼, 21¾)"

10 (10, 10, 11, 11)"

SLEEVES

piped pullover

SIZES
Sized for Man's Small, Medium, Large, X-Large. Shown in size Medium.

MEASUREMENTS
- **Chest** 45½ (49, 52½, 56)"/115.5 (124.5, 133.5, 142)cm.
- **Length** 26½ (27, 28, 28½)"/67 (68.5, 71, 72.5)cm.
- **Upper arm** 18¼ (19, 20, 21)"/46.5 (48, 50.5, 53)cm.

GAUGE
18 sts and 24 rows to 4"/10cm over St st using size 8 (5mm) needles.
Take time to check gauge.

BACK
With MC, cast on 94 (102, 110, 118) sts. Work in k2, p2 rib as foll:
Row 1 (RS) K2, *p2, k2; rep from * to end.
Row 2 P2, *k2, p2; rep from * to end.
Rep rows 1 and 2 for k2, p2 rib until piece measures 3"/7.5cm from beg, end with a WS row.
Change to CC and k 1 row, p 1 row. Change to MC, and work 16 rows in St st (k on RS, p on WS). Inc 1 st at each side on next row, then every 14th row 3 times more—102 (110, 118, 126) sts.
Work even until piece measures 16 (16, 16½, 16½)"/40.5 (40.5, 42, 42)cm from beg, end with a WS row.

Shape armhole
Bind off 4 (4, 5, 5) sts at beg of next 2 rows, 3 sts at beg of next 2 rows, 2 sts at beg of next 4 (4, 6, 6) rows. Dec 1 st at each side every other row 2 (3, 2, 4) times—76 (82, 86, 90) sts. Work even until armhole measures 8½ (9, 9½, 10)"/21.5 (23, 24, 25.5)cm, end with a WS row.

Shape shoulder and neck
Bind off 3 (3, 5, 5) sts at beg of next 6 (2, 2, 4) rows, 4 sts at beg of next 6 (10, 10, 8) rows, AT THE SAME TIME, after 4 rows of

shoulder shaping have been worked, bind off center 18 (20, 20, 22) sts for neck and working both sides at once, bind off 3 sts from neck edge twice and 2 sts once.

FRONT
Work as for back until piece measures 16 (16, 16½, 16½)"/40.5 (40.5, 42, 42)cm from beg, end with a WS row.

Shape armhole and neck
Shape armholes same as back, AT THE SAME TIME, when armhole measures 1½ (2, 2½, 3)"/4 (5, 6.5, 7.5)cm, mark center of row, and work as foll:
Next row (RS) K to 2 sts before marker, join CC and k4, join new ball of MC and work to end. Working both sides at once, work 3 more rows in St st, matching colors and cont to shape armhole.

Shape placket
Next row (RS) Work in colors as established to center, join 2nd ball of CC and work in colors as established to end. Working both sides at once, work even, keeping 2 neck edge sts each side in CC and all other sts in MC, until armhole measures 7½ (8, 8½, 9)"/19 (20.5, 21.5, 23)cm, end with a WS row.

Shape neck and shoulder
Bind off from each neck edge 4 (5, 5, 6) sts once, 4 sts once, 3 sts once, 2 sts once, dec 1 st every other row 4 times. AT THE SAME TIME, when armhole measures same as back to shoulder, shape shoulder at side edge same as back.

SLEEVES
With MC, cast on 46 sts. Work in k2, p2 rib same as back. Change to CC and k 1 row, p 1 row. Change to MC and work in St st, inc 1 st each side every 4th row 18 (20, 22, 24) times—82 (86, 90, 94) sts. Work even until piece measures 19½ (20, 20, 20½)"/49.5 (50.5, 50.5, 52)cm from beg.

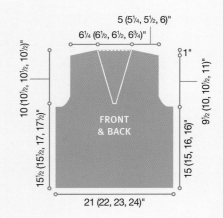

Shape cap

Bind off 4 (4, 5, 5) sts at beg of next 2 rows, 3 sts at beg of next 4 rows, 2 sts at beg of next 6 (8, 10, 12) rows, 3 sts at beg of next 6 rows and 4 (4, 3, 3) sts at beg of next 2 rows. Bind off rem 24 sts.

FINISHING

Block pieces to measurements. Sew shoulder seams.

Collar

With RS facing and CC, pick up and k 26 (27, 27, 28) sts along right front neck, 42 (44, 44, 46) sts along back neck, and 26 (27, 27, 28) sts along left front neck—94 (98, 98, 102) sts. P 1 row.

Next row (RS) With CC, k2, with MC, k to last 2 sts, with CC, k2.

Next row With CC, p2, with MC, p2, *k2, p2; rep from * to last 2 sts, with CC, p2.

Next row With CC, k2, with MC, k2, *p2, k2; rep from * to last 2 sts, with CC, k2.

Rep last 2 rows 8 times more, then rep row 2 once more.

Cut MC. With CC, k 1 row, p 1 row, then bind off all sts.

Set in sleeves. Sew side and sleeve seams.

Crochet trim

With RS facing, CC and crochet hook, work 2 adjacent rows of sl st at each armhole seam. Work in same way along shoulder seams, working from the outside in. Sew zipper into placket and collar edge. ■

father & son jackets

SIZES

Sized for Child's (4, 6, 8, 10) and Man's [Small, Medium, Large, X-Large, XX-Large]. Shown in size Child's (4) and Man's [Medium].
Note Child's sizes are in parentheses ( ), Man's sizes are in brackets [ ].

MEASUREMENTS

• **Chest (closed)** (29½, 32, 35¼, 37¾)"/(75, 81.5, 89.5, 96)cm; [43, 46, 49, 51¾, 54¾]"/ [109, 116.5, 124.5, 131.5, 139]cm.
• **Length** (16½, 17½, 18½, 20)"/(42, 44, 47, 51)cm; [24½, 25, 26, 26½, 27½]"/[62, 63.5, 66, 67.5, 69.5]cm.
• **Upper arm** (13, 14, 15, 16)"/(33, 35.5, 38, 40.5)cm; [17, 18, 19, 20, 21]"/[43.5, 46, 48.5, 51, 54]cm.

GAUGE

22 sts and 26 rows to 4"/10cm over mistake stitch rib pattern using larger needles. *Take time to check gauge.*

MISTAKE STITCH RIB

(multiple of 4 sts plus 3)
Row 1 (RS) *K2, p2; rep from * to last 3 sts, end k2, p1.
Rep row 1 for mistake stitch rib.

NOTE

Work all increases and decreases 1 st in from edge.

BACK

With larger needles, cast on (79, 87, 95, 103); [115, 123, 131, 139, 147] sts. Work in mistake stitch rib until piece measures (9, 9½, 10, 11)"/(23, 24, 25.5, 26.5)cm; [15, 15, 15½, 15½, 16]"/[38, 38, 39.5, 39.5, 40.5]cm from beg.

Shape armholes

Bind off (8, 8, 12, 12) sts; [12, 12, 16, 16, 16] sts at beg next 2 rows—(63, 71, 71, 79); [91, 99, 99, 107, 115] sts. Work even until armhole measures (6½, 7, 7½, 8)"/[16.5, 17.5,

Yarn 4

Any worsted weight wool and acrylic blend yarn
• (17½oz/500g, 880yd/810m; 21oz/600g, 1050yd/970m; 24½oz/700g, 1230yd/1130m; 28oz/800g, 1400yd/1280m) for Child's
• [38½oz/1100g, 1930yd/1770m; 42oz/1200g, 2100yd/1920m; 45½oz/1300g, 2280yd/2090m; 49oz/1400g, 2450yd/2240m; 52½oz/1500g, 2630yd/2410m] for Man's

Needles
• One pair each sizes 6 and 8 (4 and 5mm) needles *or size to obtain gauge*

Notions
• Heavy duty separating jacket zipper (16, 16, 18, 18)"/(40, 40, 45, 45)cm; [22, 24, 24, 26, 26]"/[55, 60, 60, 65, 65]cm length
• Two stitch holders
• Stitch markers
• Sewing needle and thread

19, 20.5]cm; [8½, 9, 9½, 10, 10½]"/[21.5, 23, 24, 25.5, 26.5]cm.

Shape shoulders and neck

Bind off (5, 6, 6, 7); [9, 10, 10, 11, 12] sts at beg of next 4 rows, (6, 7, 7, 8); [8, 10, 10, 11, 13] sts at beg of next 2 rows, AT THE SAME TIME, bind off center (23, 25, 25, 27); [27, 27, 27, 29, 29] sts for back neck, and working both sides at once, bind off (2); [3] sts at each neck edge twice.

RIGHT FRONT

With larger needles, cast on (41, 45, 49, 53); [61, 65, 69, 73, 77] sts.

Beg pat

Row 1 Work in mistake stitch rib to last 2 sts, k2.
Row 2 K2, work in mistake stitch rib to end.
Rep these 2 rows for pat, keeping 2 sts at front edge in garter st, until piece measures same as back to armhole shaping, end with a RS row.

Shape armhole

Bind off (8, 8, 12, 12) sts; [12, 12, 16, 16, 16] sts at beg of next WS row—(33, 37, 37, 41); [49, 53, 53, 57, 61] sts. Cont in pat until armhole measures 6 (5½, 7, 6)"/15.5 (14, 17.5, 15.5)cm; [6, 7½, 7, 8½, 8]"/15.5 [19, 17.5, 21.5, 20.5]cm, end with a WS row.

Shape front neck

Next row (RS) Work in pat over (7, 8, 8, 9); [9, 9, 9, 10, 10] sts and place on holder for front neck, work to end. Cont in pat, bind off from neck edge as foll:
For child's only—3 sts twice, 2 sts twice;
For man's only—3 sts twice, 2 sts 3 times, 1 st twice, AT THE SAME TIME,
For all sizes—when same length as back to shoulder, shape shoulder at side edge same as back.

LEFT FRONT

With larger needles, cast on (41, 45, 49, 53); [61, 65, 69, 73, 77] sts.

Beg pat

Row 1 *K2, p2; rep from * to last st, k1.
Row 2 *P2, k2; rep from * to last stitch, k1.
Rep these 2 rows for mistake stitch rib and work as for right front, reversing all shaping.

SLEEVES

With smaller needles, cast on (43); [51] sts. Work in mistake stitch rib for (1.5"/4cm); [2"/5 cm]. Change to larger needles. Cont in mistake stitch pat, inc 1 st each side, working inc sts into pat,
For child's only—every (4th, 4th, 2nd, 2nd) rows (11, 17, 4, 5) times, every (6th, 0, 4th, 4th) row (3, 0, 16, 18) times—(71, 77, 83, 89) sts;
For man's only—every [4th, 4th, 4th, 2nd, 2nd] row [8, 17, 26, 5, 9] times, every [6th, 6th, 6th, 4th, 4th] rows [13, 7, 1, 25, 23] times—[93, 99, 105, 111, 115] sts.
For all sizes—Work even until piece measures (12, 12½, 13½, 15)"/(30.5, 31.5, 34.5, 38)cm; [20]"/[51]cm from beg. Place a marker at each end of row. Work even for (1½, 1½, 2, 2)"/(4, 4, 5, 5)cm; [2, 2, 3, 3, 3]"/

MAKE MATCH-
ING SWEATERS
FOR YOUR TWO
FAVORITE GUYS!

father & son jackets

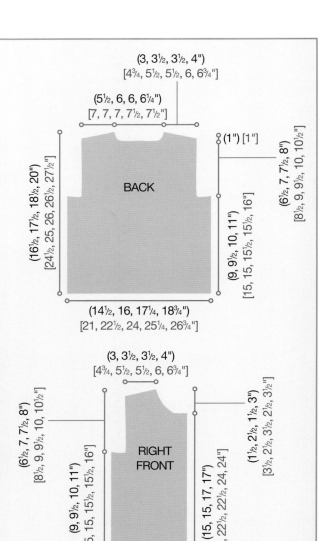

(3, 3½, 3½, 4")
[4¾, 5½, 5½, 6, 6¾"]

(5½, 6, 6, 6¼")
[7, 7, 7, 7½, 7½"]

(1") [1"]

(6½, 7, 7½, 8")
[8½, 9, 9½, 10, 10½"]

BACK

(16½, 17½, 17½, 18½, 20")
[24½, 25, 26, 26½, 27½"]

(9, 9½, 10, 11")
[15, 15, 15½, 15½, 16"]

(14½, 16, 17¼, 18¾")
[21, 22½, 24, 25¼, 26¾"]

(3, 3½, 3½, 4")
[4¾, 5½, 5½, 6, 6¾"]

(6½, 7, 7½, 8")
[8½, 9, 9½, 10, 10½"]

RIGHT FRONT

(1½, 2½, 1½, 3")
[3½, 2½, 3½, 2½, 3½"]

(9, 9½, 10, 11")
[15, 15, 15½, 15½, 16"]

(15, 15, 17, 17")
[21, 22½, 22½, 24, 24"]

(7½, 8, 9, 9½")
[11, 11¾, 12½, 13¼, 14"]

(13, 14, 15, 16")
[17, 18, 19, 20, 21"]

SLEEVES

(1½, 1½, 2, 2")
[2, 2, 3, 3, 3"]

(12, 12½, 13½, 15")
[20"]

(8") [9¼"]

[5, 5, 7.5, 7.5, 7.5]cm more. Bind off all sts loosely in pat.

FINISHING

Block pieces to measurements.
Sew shoulder seams.

Neckband

With RS facing and smaller needles, work (7, 8, 8, 9); [9, 9, 9, 10, 10] sts from right front neck holder pick up and k (67, 69, 69, 71); [87, 87, 87, 89, 89] sts evenly around neck edge, work (7, 8, 8, 9); [9, 9, 9, 10, 10] sts from left front neck holder—(81, 85, 85, 89); [105, 105, 105, 109, 109] sts.

Row 1 (WS) K2, *p2, k2; rep from * to last 3 sts, end p1, k2.
Row 2 K2, *k2, p2; rep from * to last 3 sts, end k3. Rep these 2 rows until neckband measures (1"/2.5cm); [1, 1½, 1½, 2, 2]"/[2.5, 4, 4, 5, 5]cm. Bind off loosely in rib.

FINISHING

Sew in sleeves. Sew side and sleeve seams. Sew in zipper at fronts.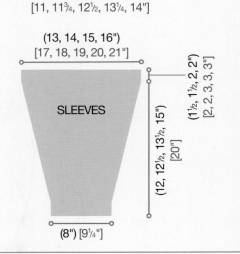